In memory of

Chaya Mierah Mindel Bas Moshe Riener, *z"l*

She illuminated the worlds of all who knew her.

Michael and Aliza Austein

એૹૹૹૹૹ

In loving memory of our dear grandparents

Max and Rose Kessler and Eddie Pollak, *a"h*

Your honesty and integrity were a constant source
of inspiration to us

May their *neshama*s have an *aliyah*
through the reading of this book

Avi and Elisheva Marciano

Dedication

To our children with all of our love

We are forever grateful for each and every one of you.
May your lives be filled with joy,
and may the worlds that you build with G-d's help
produce the most beautiful edifices,
and a legacy to last eternally.

Memorials

In loving memory of our dear father and father-in-law
Baruch ben Zev Yehuda Berger, *z"l*
Whose smile lit up the room in the darkest of times.
His love for Torah and for those who knew him will always be
remembered.

Dan and Dina Neuman

☙❧☙❧

In loving memory of
Jacob Bentolila, *z"l*
Our beloved and unforgettable uncle

Who lived his life with open hands and a sensitive heart that
manifested itself in his generosity to the poor, orphans, and the
needy, who always found his door open. He was a pure soul, a
noble and kind man, willing to go above and beyond to bring
comfort to others. A true *ozer dalim*.

May his *neshamah* have an *aliyah*.

Saadia and Shoshana Benzaquen

Contents

Preface

In my teaching and lecturing experience as a rabbi and professor of Talmudic law, a career that spans thirty-eight years, I have seen the value of using the universal language of humor to help establish a rapport with my audience and to open up their hearts and minds to the lesson to be learned. I am attempting the same with the written word. My goal is to inspire others to think and to contemplate their course in life in a way that will maximize their productivity and actualize the vast potential possessed by every human being. It is difficult to penetrate someone's heart or touch a person's soul given the many protective walls we all build. My hope is to break down those barriers by beginning each essay with a humorous story so that the reader can be engaged and then, hopefully, inspired.

This concept has, thank G-d, met with success in the three volumes of *A Time to Laugh, A Time to Listen* geared toward an Orthodox Jewish reading public, which I've been privileged to publish over the last three years. From reviews and comments received, I feel that this objective was achieved.

In this latest volume, *A Bit of Wit, a World of Wisdom*, the world edition of *A Time to Laugh, a Time to Listen*, I am attempting to present many of those same ideas in a nonsectarian format that will appeal to any thinking person, irrespective of his religious denomination. My hope is that this present collection of essays will be of interest to a broad section of the reading population – those interested in personal growth and self-development – due to its more general and non-parochial format. At the same time, my goal remains the same: to inspire the human spirit to tap into its vast potential and to expand its horizons.

It is my fervent prayer that this project meets with success, and most importantly, that it affords others the opportunity to laugh a bit, and listen a great deal, as their wisdom accrues and their worlds expand eternally.

Respectfully,
Yehoshua Kurland
January 20, 2013

Acknowledgments

All gratitude and appreciation must begin and end with the unequivocal recognition of the gift of life that G-d so graciously bestows upon us every second. I am eternally grateful to Him for that and so much more, as well as for enabling me to commit my thoughts to the written word in this latest attempt to inspire. It is my sincere hope that the words that flow from my heart will enter yours, dear readers, and will serve as a source of inspiration that engenders personal growth and inner joy.

It is with a great sense of gratitude that I offer my deepest and heartfelt appreciation to those dear students and friends who helped enable this endeavor come to fruition. They were not only forthcoming with their generosity, but with their encouragement and enthusiasm as well, which gave me great strength. I am constantly thankful to have been blessed with such wonderful students and cherish our relationships. May they be blessed with great joy in their lives together with their wives and children in good health for many long years to come.

With this in mind I extend my sincere thanks to Michael Austein of Lawrence, NY; Sadi Benzaquen of Far Rockaway, NY; Marc Friedman and Carmi Greunbaum of Lawrence, NY; Adam Kay of Far Rockaway, NY; Avi Marciano of Queens, NY; and Dan Neuman of Jerusalem, Israel, and their wives. You all have a special place in my heart.

A special thanks for their kindness in making this venture a reality goes to my dear son-in-law Yudi Walden (and of course my daughter Chaya Sara) and his dear friend (and mine) and business partner Ephraim Zagelbaum and his wife. Your magnanimous and spontaneous willingness to help is greatly treasured. May you and your families enjoy all of the blessings from Above for many long years in good health.

I will always be in debt to my revered teachers of years past and present, my colleagues, my students and friends, as well as my parents and in-laws of blessed memory. They have taught me all that I know and no doubt this present volume is a tribute to their memory.

Many thanks to a dear student and friend, Jonathan Jarashow, who made the initial contact in introducing me to Gefen Publishing House. It has been my great pleasure to work together with Gefen and their talented staff. Many thanks to my dear friend, another former student of years ago, Mr. Michael Fischberger, copublisher at Gefen, along with his partner copublisher Mr. Ilan Greenfield, for their keen understanding of my intentions in this project, and their confidence in me and my work in deeming this volume worthy of publication. A special thank you to Lynn Douek, project manager, for using her masterful organizational skills in coordinating this effort. I am deeply grateful to an extremely talented editor, Ita Olesker, for her expertise and many concrete suggestions and clarifications that will, no doubt, help make this volume abundantly clear and readable. It has been a pleasure working with all of you. Your professionalism is only outshined by your refinement and sophistication.

No words can properly express my infinite indebtedness to my partner in life, my wife, Leah. There can be no greater gift in the world than a loving and supportive wife, and you have surpassed all expectations. All that I have is in your merit, and I only pray that G-d grant us long years together to continue our united mission in life in good health, please G-d.

There can be no greater fulfillment to parents than children who are loving and devoted. Mommy and I are so very blessed to merit such a wonderful crew. You are each so special in your own right and are a pride and joy to the old folks. As a small token of appreciation for all of you, I dedicate this volume of *A Bit of Wit, A World of Wisdom* to you, my dear children. To Rivky and Yossi, Devorah, Chaya Sara and Yudi, Chani, Aryeh and Bassy, Eli and Kayla, Chaim and his *kallah* Chaya Soloveitchik, Dena and Naftali, Rissel, Shlomo, and Dovid, thank you for being exactly who you are. We can't tell you how much we love and respect you, and how proud we are of you. May you actualize all of your many talents in a way that will curry the favor of our Father in Heaven, and may you thereby merit all of His blessings.

And last but not least, I thank you, dear readers. Without you, this book might have but one reader: the author. May this volume help inspire you to take steps to improve your lot in life and make the world a better place, as you build your worlds with increased wisdom and joy.

Yehoshua Kurland
February 9, 2013
Far Rockaway, NY

A BIT OF WIT

A man went into a bookstore and asked the saleswoman: "Where is the self-help section?"

She answered: "If I tell you, it would defeat the whole purpose!"

A World of Wisdom

If I am not for myself, who will be for me?
And if I am only for myself, what am I?
And if not now, when?

(Ethics of Our Fathers 1:14)

Introduction

Communication is a powerful tool that allows us to learn from our fellow man and thereby expand our horizons. Communication comes in different forms and shapes and is not restricted to verbal articulation. It can be a facial expression or a physical gesture, which may say more than a long essay or lecture. Sometimes it's the passion and the emotion of expression, or the tone and decibel. Although no doubt the spoken word between those who share a common language and vernacular is most likely to succeed in transmitting an idea with maximal absorption, nonetheless, at times even people who are lacking in linguistic communication skills can enjoy a high-level, effective communicatory relationship.

One form of communication that all would agree is universal is the language of humor. It is a medium of expression that breaks down barriers. It has an uncanny power to unite two parties, one to the other, to absorb and to reveal, creating an atmosphere of comfort that eases the tension and opens up the heart. A light matter, a bit of laughter, a smile on one's lips slowly but surely remove all the barriers that otherwise immobilize and impede the lines of communication.

Much has been written about the benefits of laughter. From the domain of physical and mental health to social integration, this manifestation of joy brings much positive gain. Purportedly, laughter boosts immunity, lowers stress hormones, decreases pain, relaxes one's muscles, prevents heart disease, eases anxiety and fear, and adds joy and zest to life. In addition, it helps diffuse conflict, strengthens relationships, and promotes group bonding. It has been referred to as strong medicine for mind and body. But what about the soul? Can this powerful emotion be used as a tool in spiritual pursuits? Indeed it can!

King Solomon, the wisest of all men, made use of the parable in his classic book of Proverbs, in a way that penetrated the heart and pierced through all barriers. The simplicity of the metaphor drives home the most profound teaching by first establishing a rapport of sorts that allows the message to seep in slowly but surely, until its deeper meaning is absorbed. When a concept is distant from us, we need to comprehend it initially via a medium to which we can relate, and ultimately we will compare one thing to another until we perceive the depth of the matter.

Many a censure or a gentle reprimand is inevitably detached from us – or we make sure it is by blocking all entries. Too delicate and too fragile to allow such poignant words to permeate our being, we build "walls of protection." But in truth these walls don't protect us at all. Quite to the contrary, they destroy us. They prevent us from listening with an open ear and an open heart to allow us to make the proper adjustments, to change and to grow.

The genius of the parable is that it is not construed as a threat, and we thereby don't fight it. Instead, we open ourselves up to its message, subconsciously tearing down the walls of interference. A good story can act in this capacity as well. It relaxes the listener and inspires an openness that permits communication.

A humorous story that additionally serves as a parable has an added advantage in that the comic relief and mirthful spirit generated in its wake inspires an even greater openness. Laughter can replace narrowness with roominess, as the listener evolves into a vessel able to receive. The classic light matter combined with a parable is a winning combination that can open hearts, peel away barricades, and permit profound communication.

It has been my hope from the beginning that the words that are expressed from my heart enter your hearts, dear readers. But hearts are not easily entered. Perhaps with a bit of laughter, those chambers will respond. Such is my fervent prayer on the writing of the first volume of this humble attempt to inspire. And although I expect many comments that will range from: "I read your book from cover to cover – actually I only read the jokes," to "please send me A Bit of Wit only. I'm not interested in the A World of Wisdom part," I am confident that most of you will perceive precisely what I am trying to achieve through the medium of humor. Let us join ranks in heart and soul as we laugh together, but more importantly, listen, with an open ear and open heart that inspires the building of worlds replete with wisdom.

King David writes in Psalms: "And they shall rejoice with trepidation." Indeed these two very powerful emotions can not only coexist, but complement one another, when they combine to inspire serious contemplation that generates growth and change. It is my ardent hope that our laughter will inspire a loosening of our inhibitions, so that we break down those walls of encumbrance and internalize the lessons to be learned from these essays – to reach spiritual heights never imagined.

Everyone enjoys a good laugh. Humor is a universal language that helps lighten the burden and opens up the heart. Yet the joy generated through a good joke is temporary at best. However, when it helps teach an important lesson for life, that joy can be eternal.

BETWEEN
Man
and G-d

Answering to a Higher Authority

DEVELOPING FEAR OF HEAVEN LEADS TO LONG, HEALTHY, AND PRODUCTIVE YEARS.

Bernie was a good and pious man. When he passed away, G-d Himself greeted him in Heaven and asked if he would like something to eat.

"I could eat something," replied Bernie. So G-d opened up a can of chunk light tuna, and they shared it.

While eating his humble meal, Bernie looked down in the underworld. He noticed the inhabitants there were devouring enormous steaks, pheasant, pastries, and scotch, Johnny Walker Blue Label no less.

The next day, G-d approached Bernie and asked if he was hungry. Bernie, again, answered in the affirmative.

Once again, a can of tuna was opened and shared, while down below, Bernie couldn't help but notice a feast of caviar, champagne, lamb chops, truffles, brandy, and chocolates.

The next day, mealtime arrived, and another can of tuna was opened.

Meekly, Bernie approached G-d and said, "I don't get it! My whole life I sacrificed to develop fear of Heaven so that one day I would merit a place in Heaven. Now I'm here, and all I get to eat is tuna! But in that other place, they eat gourmet meals like kings! I just don't understand!"

"To be honest," G-d replied, "for just the two of us, it doesn't pay to cook."

CSCREOBO

One of life's most difficult achievements is to develop a fear of a Higher Authority. In a world that champions independence and the free spirit, we fear nothing, let alone the abstract. *Time* magazine took care of G-d a long time ago when they so audaciously displayed the headline on their cover "Is G-d Dead?" When one adds to that man's preoccupation with self-worship, enamored as he is by the accomplishments of "his own strength" and "his own hand," acknowledgment of any Supreme Power becomes a major challenge.

Theories abound as to the world's origin, some more scientific than others, yet all still theories. The overwhelming feeling one experiences of a force far greater than oneself, or the natural hush that inevitably results among those privileged to marvel at the sight of the Grand Canyon or Niagara Falls, attests to a pure and pristine inner voice that whispers, "There is much beyond your limited existence that transcends worlds beyond this one." Any person who has witnessed the miracle of childbirth as a new life emerges is immediately swept up with a feeling of awe and humility. The weak and the infirm most certainly understand their limitations as mere mortals and their reliance upon a power that is All-Knowing and All-Powerful. Life's experiences are replete with inspiration that will lead a person on the path of fear of Heaven, if only he will open his eyes to see.

Poor Bernie! He's up there in Heaven all by himself. Let us strive to open our hearts to stand in awe of G-d, and after many long, healthy, and productive years on this earth, we, and the many we inspire along the way, will join him for a gourmet dinner eternally.

Busted

The two college students overdid it the Sunday night before the big final and overslept the next morning. Too late to make the test, they decided on a "story" they would tell the professor. Having carefully rehearsed the drama, they told of their courageous effort to drive back in the torrential rain from visiting one of the student's aging grandparents over the weekend. They had left early with plenty of time to spare, but had gotten a flat tire and were stranded for hours without a spare on a secluded country road until help arrived.

The professor listened carefully and calmly told them that they could take a make-up test the next morning at 9:00 a.m. Happy that their little "story" had worked, they were there bright and early the next morning. The professor handed them their test booklets and placed them in separate rooms. The first essay question was worth 5 points and was quite easy, prompting them to think that the test would be a breeze.

Then they turned to question two: "95 points – Which tire was it?"

∞∞∞∞∞

Getting caught is not fun, but on the bright side it has the power to shock us into reality. Whether we are outright liars or merely clever "rationalizers," we can go on bending the truth endlessly, convinced that we are being honest and straightforward. It can literally take shock treatment to shake us from our self-imposed oblivion, to convert our heartbeat to the rhythm of truth. The "white lies" of our youth can easily evolve into the "big lies" of an adulthood that is plagued with inconsistency. Society has taught us well to "get away with what you can," and we risk developing into chronic fabricators, a life-threatening disease.

The wording of the instruction in Scripture, "From a matter of falsehood, you shall distance yourself," suggests more than just a command, but a prediction as well. From even one matter of false-hood, you shall indeed fall farther and farther away from the truth, as this bad habit subtly unravels. From instructing our children to tell the person calling on the phone that we are not home (or even "not available," when we really are), to cheating on our taxes, the tragic game continues until somewhere along the line, the "fabrica-tor" finally gets "busted." Years ago, there was a game show, This is Your Life, where the contestant would tell his life story and would be rewarded by a surprise visit from someone dear and significant to him from his youth. The reunion was marked by a flood of emotions. I sarcastically envisioned a similar game show where the visitor from the past was the guy he cut off on the expressway or the fellow whose parking space he stole. Imagine the impact of that meeting!

I was once ticketed for passing a school bus. I was sure that the bus driver had waived me on. The police officer, however, saw it dif-ferently. I decided to fight the ticket. I prepared my defense, including a letter from the very owner of the bus company (who happened to be my next door neighbor) vouching for me. I went to court hoping the officer would not show up. Sure enough there he was. As I stood before the judge, who reminded me of the former head of the KKK, the police officer promptly stated his case, making me sound like the world's most wanted criminal. I thought it was all over. Then a miracle occurred. Without even asking for my defense, the judge declared, "Insufficient evidence, case dismissed!" I left as quickly as I could, before the judge could change his mind. I sure was happy that I'd never have to see that police officer again.

A full year and a half later, my daughter, driving my leased car, was stopped by the police and accused of driving a stolen car. I quickly raced to the scene to explain to the officers that the car wasn't even mine, but rather was a lease. Fortunately they believed my story and asked if I could wait a few days before contacting the leasing company as they wanted to investigate. They told me that a detective would come to visit me at my home just to get the information. I agreed, and they promptly impounded the car.

Two days later, a plain-clothed detective came to my house together with another uniformed police officer who happened to be driving with him. As we stood in the kitchen of my house, the detective gathered the information he needed, which of course included my name, when suddenly his companion burst out: "Hey! I know that name! Why, you're the guy who passed the school bus! You're so lucky that the judge had it out for me!" There he was, right in my own kitchen, the man I thought I'd never have to face again, three-dimensional and in full color.

The sages speak of a day that seems to be even more concerning than the Day of Judgment, and that is the Day of Rebuke. Could there be anything more worrisome than the Day of Judgment? After a Day of Judgment, what need is there for a Day of Rebuke? It has been suggested that the former refers to an assessment of a person's actual performance (his deeds and misdeeds), whereas the latter refers to the total refutation of all the excuses and justifications, the rationalizations and the lies, deliberate or unintentional. As he explains to the Heavenly Court why his constricted finances didn't allow him to give the donation to charity on the third of September, he will be shown the $150 receipt from Radio Shack for the latest iPod, dated the third of September. The examples can get worse and more embarrassing. The point is well understood. We can't fool ourselves forever.

Most importantly, we need to recognize that G-d's signet is truth, and therefore we should strive to emulate Him in the very matter He has chosen as His badge of honor. We can well understand why a falsehood creates distance, for it distances us from G-d's very essence. At the same time it rings clear how when truth becomes the symbol of our identity, we unite with our Creator in creed, as we seal our fate with the stamp of eternity.

Has Anyone Seen My Father?

EACH PERSON'S CONTRIBUTION TO THE WORLD IS ONE THAT IS SINGULARLY THEIRS.

A man approached the ringmaster of the circus, hoping to join the circus as a lion tamer.

"Do you have any experience?" the ringmaster asked.

"Do I have experience? Why of course! My father, of blessed memory, was a world-famous lion tamer," the man exclaimed. "He taught me everything he knew."

"Really?" said the ringmaster. "Did he teach you how to make a lion jump through a flaming hoop?"

"Oh! Absolutely," he responded.

"Have you ever had six lions form a pyramid?" the ringmaster continued.

"Oh, that's my favorite!" he answered enthusiastically.

Quite impressed, the circus leader pressed on. "Have you ever stuck your head in a lion's mouth?"

"Just once," he answered.

"Why only once?" the ringmaster inquired.

The man answered, "I was looking for my father!"

ଔଔଔଔଔ

The legacy of a person's ancestry is not purely historical. It links the past with the present and helps a person understand his unique mission in life. We must look to our father and mother, grandparents and great-grandparents, to help us perceive our place in history and our innate talents and potential. Connecting to our past not only fills us with pride and boosts our confidence, it inspires us to focus on the idea that man is not an island unto himself, but rather a link in the chain of destiny. It impacts us to do our utmost to contribute our portion to improve the world and advance the productivity of mankind.

No two people are alike, both in the physical and spiritual sense. Just as their bodies are heterogeneous, so are their souls. Each person's contribution to the world is one that is singularly theirs, and their task in life is to uncover that special talent and allow it expression. History has shown how individual people have changed the shape of the world for the better in ways that are unfathomable. And although most of us will contribute in a less magnanimous fashion, nonetheless, it would be a crime to squash that potential and leave that source of positive energy untapped and dormant. Our legacy will be that contribution, and it will live on long after our departure from this earthly existence.

It Ain't Just Luck

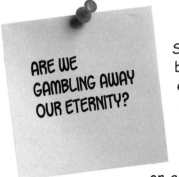

ARE WE GAMBLING AWAY OUR ETERNITY?

Steve leaves his Upper West Side brownstone at 777 West 77th St. at exactly 7:00 a.m. to catch the 7:07 Seventh Avenue Express. On his way to the train, at the corner of 7th Avenue and 77th St., he notices a manila envelope with no name or address on the ground before him. Curious about its contents, he quickly picks it up and finds it filled with $100 bills. Frantically, he counts them, amazed at his good fortune to have found $7,700.

"Today must be my lucky day!" he exclaims in delight, seven being his lucky number.

Steve stuffs the cash into his pockets and, having missed his train, hails a cab instead to complete his commute to his office at 77 7th Ave. His excitement is further intrigued when the cab driver pulls up in front of his building and tells him the fare is exactly $7.77.

"Today must be my lucky day!" he shouts out again. "I'm not going to work! I'm going to the racetrack! Driver, take me to Belmont Park Racetrack in Long Island!"

Steve is further encouraged when, upon arriving at Belmont, the taxi fare comes to exactly $77.77. "There's no doubt about it! Today is my lucky day!" he rings out, as he rushes in to place his bet. There it is on the charts. Seventh Heaven is running at the odds of seven to one in the seventh race.

"$7,777 on Seventh Heaven in the seventh race," he orders the teller, positive that today is his lucky day, and seven is his lucky number.

Sure enough, she comes in 7th!

Invariably, in the superficial existence of a shallow world devoid of depth and meaning, good-luck charms and rabbit's feet are popularly cherished. That world's notion of something a little more "esoteric" might be one's Zodiac sign, perceived as a source for predicting character or innate tendencies. "Hi, I'm a Leo!" "Hi, I'm a Gemini!" and, presto, a match made in heaven! Chinese fortune cookies are still a favorite part of the menu in Chinese restaurants. Las Vegas and Atlantic City have gained enormously from such shallowness, which unfortunately has made a major contribution to gambling addictions and the like. Behavior steeped in chance and risk taking runs the gamut from playing the stock market to every conceivable sporting event, from the sophisticated to the contemptible. To our dismay, this happy-go-lucky approach toward life has become the norm for many, and superficiality and shallow thinking reign supreme. Anything profound has been lost in a sea of casual randomness.

Life, devoid of destiny, becomes one of chance and haphazardness. It is no wonder that many are caught up in a world of adventure and risk. From bungee jumping to snowboarding, from jet skiing to parasailing and skydiving, from binge eating to alcohol consumption and substance abuse, people often engage in thrill-seeking and dangerous activities, banking on their frivolous "E-Z Pass" philosophy of living for the moment and reveling in good-luck charms.

The gambler is not only guilty of fantasy living and not pursuing gainful employment in the practical sense, but more importantly, he grossly misunderstands his unique and important mission: that of bettering his world. He is preoccupied with the foolishness of chance, when his investments should be in the futures of this world and the next. We dare not gamble away our eternal reward for a thrill or two. Our stocks and securities are our good deeds and their merit, and are not on the table for any wager whatsoever.

Impaired Vision

Marty and his wife, Sadie, hadn't spoken in days. Each was stubborn, neither wanting to give in.

But now, Marty had a dilemma: Tomorrow was the big fishing trip with Phil, and he needed to wake up early to make sure he'd make it on time. Heavy sleeper that he was, he desperately wanted to ask his wife to awaken him at 5:00 a.m. so he'd make his 5:30 departure, but he didn't want to be the first to break the silence. How could he get her to do this favor for him without "giving in"? He decided to leave a note asking her to please wake him up at 5:00 a.m.

The next morning Marty overslept and didn't wake up until 9:30. Realizing that he'd missed his ride, he frantically looked for his wife, furious at her for not waking him. All he found was a note: "Good morning! It's 5:00 a.m."

❧☙❧☙

Man is blind to his own shortcomings. He may easily see them in others, yet is often foolishly ignorant of his own inadequacies. Subjectivity is a malaise that has a cataract effect, impairing the vision of even the most astute and wise. It leaves its victims astounded and disappointed, as their expectations are inevitably not met as a result of their delusional self-imposed blindness. Subjectivity is so overwhelming that it precludes the possibility of any awareness or cognizance of its presence. It has been the beginning of the end for many a politician or public figure by virtue of a kickback of some sort, and can easily turn altruism into greed, and selflessness into a facade that in reality is self-serving.

Stubborn subjectivity has most certainly been the culprit of the communication breakdown so characteristic of relationships gone sour, when instead of a couple growing closer and becoming broader from the inevitable variances to be expected between any two human beings, neither party hears what the other has to say because they can't hear anyone but themselves.

How do we ensure that our vision is not impaired and our minds are not twisted by this destructive force? One suggestion is to make it our business to seek the advice of others in our daily routine. A solid relationship with a mentor, good friends who care, and of course a loving relationship and good communication with one's spouse are not only indispensable in overcoming the many vicissitudes that life has to offer, but help safeguard against falling into the pit of subjective thinking. In a world that at times seems to champion a lifestyle of independence and non-commitment, the wise person must know that having no one to contend with but one's pet breeds this malaise and cultivates it.

Man needs to hear the ideas of others to ensure that he is not caught up in the web of subjectivity. I say this not because it is my belief, but based on the advise of so many great people I have spoken to. Take it to heart. It will make you ever the greater, ever the wiser.

Timelessness

A man was having a conversation with G-d.

"Tell me, G-d," the man said, "how long is a million years to You?"

"A million years is like a second," G-d said.

"And how much is a million dollars to You?" the man asked.

"A million dollars is like a penny," G-d said.

Sheepishly, the man asked, "Do you think I could have a million dollars?"

G-d replied, "Sure, no problem! It will just take a second!"

CﾞꙨꙌ

In G-d's great humility, He permits Himself to be referred to in anthropomorphic terms. For example, the Scriptures often mention G-d's "hand" or G-d's "mouth." When misunderstood, these human-like expressions could contribute to a gross distortion: that there exists an equivalency and compatibility between our limited world and His.

Although He graciously created us in His image and therefore we have great potential, nonetheless, we are still mere mortals confined by time and space, with limited understanding, while G-d's world is timeless and endless, with no past, present, or future. In His world, the big picture is the only picture; it is the whole picture, the true picture. What appears to us, at times, as chaotic and confusing is a symmetrical and harmonious symphony in His world.

14

Instead of the jumbled and disorderly multicolor threads of yarn seen through our myopic vision on the underside of the tapestry, G-d sees the magnificent blend of color and design of those threads interacting in perfect sync, as they carry out His will to formulate a breathtaking scene.

G-d's mastery of orchestration leaves no room for questions of why bad things happen to good people or the like, when it is abundantly clear to us how narrow our vision is in comparison to His. A million years, to Him, are a mere second. A million dollars to Him are a mere penny. And a million questions have but one answer – the Oneness of all that has ever existed; the King of all kings. For it is He Who is all-knowing and timeless; it is He Who is the Master composer and we are mere plebeians. It is foolish for a human being to think that he can know all the answers, or any of them for that matter.

Yet we believe with absolute faith that the more we emulate His ways and actualize that vast potential to be like Him, the more we will merit comprehending the bigger picture, in this world and the next.

You're Never Alone

G-D IS ACCESSIBLE 24/7.

The city slicker ran his car off the isolated country road into a ditch. Luckily, a farmer on a wagon happened by with his big old horse named Betsy.

The man asked the farmer who he could call for help, to which the farmer replied, "Why, old Betsy here could pull that there car out of the ditch in a cinch."

The sophisticated city slicker didn't believe it for a minute, but he was stuck, so he just watched as the farmer promptly unhitched old Betsy from the wagon and attached her to the bumper of the car.

Then the farmer yelled out: "Pull Nellie, pull! You can do it!" Old Betsy didn't move.

Then he screamed out: "C'mon, Ranger, pull! Pull it out!" Betsy still did not move.

He then yelled out at the top of his lungs: "Pull, Speedster, pull!" Again Betsy just stood there.

At that point, the farmer nonchalantly said, "Okay, Betsy, pull her out!" In a matter of seconds old Betsy pulled the car out of the ditch.

Appreciative, yet curious, the city man asked the farmer why he hadn't simply called the horse by its real name immediately.

The farmer explained. "Y'all don't understand. You see, old Betsy here is blind. If she thought for a moment that she was pulling on her own, she wouldn't even try!"

L ife is filled with challenges that are difficult, and man is in need of a support system that will help him get past the hurdles. Parents and grandparents, one's spouse and children, in addition to friends and mentors, help satisfy that need. But not every person is fortunate enough to enjoy the privilege of such reassurance. Even if an individual has merited a network of support, invariably there are times when he or she feels alone. There are situations when one is close to despair and does not know where to turn for help. There certainly are undertakings that one would never attempt if he thought he were acting alone.

From a spiritual standpoint, little would be accomplished if we were convinced that we act independently, without Divine intervention and mediation. We must be resolute in our trust that we are never acting alone, for G-d is accessible 24/7, and more than willing to help us in our pursuit of holiness and all that is pure. Faith in G-d demands no less. For that matter, there isn't a breath that transpires without the intervention of Heaven. Is it any wonder, then, that He supplies us with all types of help in various times of need and is constantly at our side?

This thought finally registered within me during the many months that my father, of blessed memory, existed purely by virtue of a respirator that breathed for him. For hours I would watch the numbers on the machine that recorded the amount of breaths the machine supplied for him, and marvel at the fact that an invention of mankind could, in effect, breathe life into a person. Then it hit me. G-d is our ventilator, endlessly breathing oxygen into our bloodstream, never tiring, and not subject to the dangers of a power shortage. His Divine intervention is apparent every second.

And with this knowledge fixed prominently in our hearts and minds, we can rest assured that there are no spiritual vistas that are not ours to conquer, for indeed, we are never alone!

BETWEEN
Man
and Himself

Life Savings

For close to fifty years, Morris and his wife Esther would go to the annual state fair, and every year when passing the helicopter ride, Morris would say, "Esther, I'd really like to ride in that helicopter."

Esther would always reply, "I know, Morris, but that ride costs fifty dollars, and fifty dollars is fifty dollars!" This went on for many years.

One year, Esther and Morris went to the fair, and Morris said, "Esther, I'm eighty-five years old. If I don't take that helicopter ride now, I might never get another chance!"

Again Esther replied, "Morris, that helicopter ride cost fifty bucks, and fifty bucks is fifty bucks!"

The pilot overheard the older couple's conversation and made an offer. "Listen here, folks. I'll make you a deal. I'll take you both for a ride for free, on the condition you stay quiet the entire ride and do not say a word. But if you say one word, it'll cost you fifty bucks."

Morris and Esther agreed and up they went. The pilot put on quite a show doing all kinds of maneuvers, from the "topsy-turvy" to the "around-the-world," but not a word was heard. He did his daredevil tricks over and over again, but still not a word.

When they landed, the pilot turned half-way around to Morris and said, "By golly, I did everything I could to get you guys to yell, but you didn't utter a word. I'm impressed!"

Morris replied, "Well, to tell you the truth, I almost said something fifteen minutes ago when Esther fell out of the helicopter, but you know, fifty bucks is fifty bucks!"

21

If people would only cherish good deeds the way they hold on to their money, it would truly be a "life savings" (their own!). Any astute entrepreneur will tell you that the real value of money lies in its power of investment. To the enterprising person with a true worldview, the only eternal and universally accepted currency is the one born out of the merits of one's good deeds. It is those merits that become our eternal "credit cards," which have no expiration dates.

Man, a composite of all that was created, is a microcosm of the larger world around him. His task on this earth is to expand and branch out, so that he utilizes his innate strengths and capabilities to build his own miniature world. This world is comprised of his children and grandchildren, his students and his colleagues, the people with whom he interacts in his daily life, and all of his spiritual achievements, both between himself and G-d, and himself and his fellow. The more he works on himself, the more good deeds he performs, the more he refines his character, the more he reaches out to others, the more he escapes his natural tendency to become enslaved to a self-serving incarceration – the more glorious the world that he builds. And the more glorious a world he builds on this earth, the more beautiful an edifice he will have built eternally.

The following story says it all.

It was a hot summer's day and young Sammy was quite bored. All his friends were away in camp, and he had nobody to play with. He stood outside, throwing a ball against the garage door, hoping that when his dad got home from work he would be able to play ball with him.

The scene switches to Sammy's father, driving home in bumper-to-bumper traffic on the dreaded Van Wyck Expressway. It had been a difficult day at the office; the heat outside was oppressive, and the car air-conditioner was on the blink. To make matters worse, he had a ton of work to do once he got home. Needless to say, he was not in a good mood when he turned into his driveway, having spent a torturous extra hour and a half in traffic, sweating bullets all the way.

Sammy greeted his father with great enthusiasm. "Dad, hi! I've been waiting for you to come home all day! I'm so bored! Can we play ball together?"

"Son, I'd love to play ball with you but I've had quite a day, and I still have tons of work to do. Why don't you call a friend?"

"They're all in camp," Sammy replied.

"I'm sorry, Sammy, but I just can't right now! Please try to understand!" And with that, Sammy's father rushed into the house, took out a cold drink from the fridge, and went into his office to get down to work.

Five minutes later, Sammy was at the study door: "Dad, please. Can't we play ball for ten minutes?"

"Son, I thought I explained it to you. I'm just swamped with work. Maybe another time."

A few minutes later, Sammy returned, this time whimpering and nagging, and he said: "Please, Dad, all I want is five minutes. Can't we play ball for five minutes?"

"The answer is no! Now don't bother me anymore!" Sammy's father answered, obviously irritated.

Nonetheless, the persistent kid was back a few minutes later, whining in a sing-song fashion: "It's not fair! I've been waiting all day. Pleeeease!"

At this point, Sammy's father had had enough. He was hot and stressed out and just couldn't take his son's nagging anymore. On his desk there happened to be a magazine opened to a picture of the map of the world. In his frustration and anger, he tore out that page, ripped it into hundreds of little pieces, threw it on the floor, and exclaimed, "Son, when you can put that back together, I'll have time to play ball with you. Now do you understand? Now get lost!"

Fifteen minutes later, the kid was back: "Dad! Can we play ball now? I did what you said. I glued the page back together."

"You did what?" Sammy's father interrupted. "How in the world did you do that? Why, I tore that page into hundreds of pieces. How did you manage to paste it back together?"

Sammy responded: "Dad, you don't understand. You see, on the other side of the picture of the map of the world, there was a picture of a little boy, and if you put together the little boy, then you've put together the whole world!"

Odd Man Out

For some peculiar reason which he never understood, his parents had given him the most unusual name. They had named him "Odd." Growing up with that stigma was not easy. Suffice it to say, the other kids made life miserable for Odd by poking fun at his name.

Nonetheless, Odd persevered and learned how to deal with their ridicule, at times even laughing along with them. He went on to excel at his studies and eventually graduated from a prestigious law school and succeeded in his chosen career. He married a charming woman, and together they built a beautiful family of children and grandchildren who were their pride and joy. However, the eccentric name his parents had selected for him never ceased to bother him, and he remained disturbed by this his entire life.

As he waxed old, into his eighties, and was preparing his last will and testament, Odd made a monumental decision. He was finally going to do something about his name. He gave clear instructions that upon his death, his monument should remain free of any inscription.

Sure enough, at the ripe age of eighty-seven he passed away, and months later a monument was erected on his grave with absolutely no words etched upon it, exactly as he had requested.

And over the years, any time visitors would pass by his grave and see that bare monument, empty of words, they'd invariably comment, "That's odd!"

The name a person makes for himself on this earth will remain with him forever. That name is a product of his eternal achievements during the course of his lifetime. His accumulated merits are his ticket to eternity and will become his passport and identity there. If instead he chooses to pervert his precious years on this earth with wasteful and destructive impropriety, he will take that name to wherever he is going and have to face the music accordingly.

Not only is a "good name," comprised of the accumulation of his meritorious deeds, eternal, but its effect will continue to function with animation and vitality long after his death, through the fruits of his labor. The Sages of the Talmud say that a child is the "feet" of his deceased parents when he follows in their righteous ways. He allows them to "walk" among the dead, and to ascend from strength to strength. Similarly, a student, inspired by his mentor, continues to advance his teacher posthumously. For that matter, all fortunate recipients of positive influence continue to promote the spiritual ascent of the numerous "teachers" who inspired them during the course of their lives.

Indeed, the name we make for ourselves will remain with us long after we leave this world. We want to make sure that we build a name of which we will be proud; one that is replete with good deeds and kindness; one that will give tremendous satisfaction to our Creator, and most importantly, one that will be eternally productive. We dare not create a flawed name for ourselves that will haunt us in the world of absolute truth because of its embarrassing accomplishments, for then it will be too late, and we will be stained with that "odd" stigma forever.

Playing with a Full Deck

Man to a psychiatrist: "Doctor you've got to help me! I keep thinking that I'm a deck of cards!"

Psychiatrist: "Sit over there, and I'll deal with you later!"

ෆ෧෪෨ඐ

The world we live in today is plagued with so much emotional upheaval that at times even the well-adjusted people wonder if they are 100 percent stable. The many challenges of life, and the ever-changing turbulence of our existence, contribute to our insecurities and make us contemplate if we are, in fact, "playing with a full deck." Every Tom, Dick, and Harry has been in some form of therapy, and if he hasn't, there might be even more reason for concern. Gone are the days when getting help is a stigma, and thankfully many have been rehabilitated in the process.

But there is grave danger that lurks beneath the surface. It is the danger of man losing sight of his real potential as he relegates himself to some limited being, emotionally dependent on others, who cannot deal with situations on his own. He can easily lose confidence, as he succumbs to a mindset that renders escape from reality socially acceptable and tolerable. With all due respect to the many capable and altruistic professionals, and to those who are in fact emotionally compromised and in need of assistance, we still have to know with confidence that, fundamentally, G-d instilled in us the ability to reach within ourselves and procure a surge of strength to tackle the ups and downs of life. Through the structure of our religious beliefs and the guidance and council of our mentors and role models, through working on the improvement of our character traits in a systematic way, we can stand up to the challenges that face us and emerge strong in mind and soul, ready to take on the world.

Although it goes without saying that when there are real problems, they need to be attended to by mental health professionals, nonetheless I wonder: To what degree have we caved in to the mores of a bankrupt society and become dependent upon counseling professionals for emotional support, because of a lack of any depth or meaning in our lives? Wellsprings of strength and resources to deal with life's disappointments lie deeply inside of each person, if only he or she would reach for them. When instead, we give up immediately and depend on others to get us through the tough times, we lose touch with those innate sources of strength with which we were provided, and emotional atrophy sets in.

A well-known comedian's quip about paying his psychologist comes to mind. He reasoned, upon being handed the $500 invoice for his visit: "Why should I pay him $500 for telling me that perhaps I'm not really me? Why, if I'm not me, maybe he's not him, and if that's so, why should I pay him for services that he didn't provide?"

Indeed, if somehow we could tap into the reserve that G-d gave us that is uniquely ours and use it to face the challenges of life – if we could remain in touch with the "real me" – we wouldn't need those professional services in the first place. By no means do I mean to suggest that one shouldn't ask advice, nor do I mean to minimize the importance of consulting with a mentor, or at times seeking out professional intervention, but never should we forget that G-d gave us the means to deal with life's travails, and with a little adjustment here and there, we can tap into those resources.

William Shakespeare said it best: "This above all: to thine own self be true." Your "own self" is more equipped to deal with the vicissitudes of life than you might think. You can do it! Yes you can!

PRIORITIES

SETTING PRIORITIES MEANS RELINQUISHING MANY OF THE ENCHANTMENTS OF ONE'S HEART.

Bernie was shocked to see an empty seat in the row ahead of him at the Super Bowl. Feeling somewhat bold, he asked the woman seated next to the empty seat, "Excuse me, but whose seat is that?"

"Oh! That's my husband's seat," the woman replied.

"Well, where is he?" Bernie inquired, perhaps overstepping his bounds. "He'll miss the kickoff!"

The lady answered, "Oh, he passed away!"

"I'm terribly sorry," Bernie lamented, silently scolding himself for allowing his curiosity to get the better of him and acting so nosy. But never one to control his mouth, he persisted. "Excuse me for asking one more question. Didn't any of your relatives want the seat?"

"Oh, no!" the lady answered. "They all insisted on going to the funeral!"

⋙⋘

Misplaced priorities, you might say, at its worse. Yet at times, we are not far behind in our distorted hierarchy of precedence and preference. Growing up in an affluent society, we develop many loves and interests, all of which quickly become part of our very being and find a warm spot in our hearts. Parting from them or even relegating them to a lower position on our priority chart becomes quite difficult. It is impossible to establish a true measure of one's priorities when everything is important. In addition, we live in an environment in which many people want it all and are used to getting everything they want. This invariably leads to a situation where the truly crucial areas of life are unfairly shared with the less significant ones.

Life is replete with decision making. It demands weighing one thing against another in order to determine which direction to go, which direction will maximize productivity and gain. We are constantly making choices, and we desperately need a system of priorities to serve as a structure that will help us strike the proper balance and protect us from overemphasizing the insignificant and underestimating that which is crucial.

The person who has an important job interview at 9:00 in the morning in Manhattan must choose to go to sleep early the night before rather than party until the wee hours of the morning. Landing that job is critical to his happiness and that of his family. He can celebrate on another occasion. Placing aside one thing for another, however, becomes difficult when one's heart is enchanted with it all. We have been the fortunate beneficiaries of an affluent society which lacks nothing. But there are drawbacks to having it all, and this is one of them. Life's decisions are too important to allow the indulgence of our youth to interfere with the wisdom and perspicacity essential to making the right choices.

We live at a time when it is necessary to inscribe messages on the flaps of boxes of candy that plead with children to "say no to drugs." Choices that years ago were far-gone conclusions are now legitimate concerns and alternatives for all too many. Substance abuse and behavior that is destructive and debilitating, licentious and promiscuous, fill the streets and invade the privacy of our homes. We even invite these influences into our lives without reservation. Is there no structure to our lives? Have we no standards? Or as the author Manis Friedman once put it: "Doesn't anyone blush anymore?"

Of course we would like to make the right decisions, but we need help. We must have a system, a code, a structure, that speaks truth and common sense. Otherwise we are left on our own, too awestruck by the dazzle – too "in love" with it all – to make courageous decisions that are sensible and futuristic, mature and enduring. We dare not trust our own, self-devised priority system. We could spend the best years of our lives seizing the inessential and even destructive, and relinquishing the perpetual and immortal.

Short-Term Sacrifice, for Long-Term Gain

WE ARE ALL IN OLYMPIC TRAINING FOR THE ULTIMATE GOLD MEDAL.

A businessman on a trip to India arrived at the airport in New Delhi. He took a taxi to his hotel, where he was greeted by his hospitable Indian host. The cab driver requested the equivalent of eighteen U.S. dollars for the fare. It seemed reasonable, so the American started to hand him the money.

The Indian host, enraged by what he thought was a classic case of a cab driver taking advantage of a naïve visitor, grabbed the bills and initiated a verbal assault on the cabby, calling him a "parasite" and a "disgrace to his country" for trying to overcharge visitors. The host then threw half the amount at the driver and told him never to return!

As the taxi sped off, the host gave the visitor the remaining bills and said: "Sorry about that! Now, how was your trip?"

"Fine," answered the American. "It was all going so well, until you chased the cab away with my luggage in the trunk."

❧✽❀✽❧

Successful investment bankers and financiers have a keen sense for a good deal, with an uncanny ability to be fiscally futuristic and clairvoyant. At times it would seem that they are almost prophetic in their intuitions and premonitions. But man's ability to be insightful was not given to him to enrich him in this world, as much as to enhance his eternity. G-d enjoins us: "Make good investments!"

A little sacrifice in this world will go a long way in the World to Come. What we might deem as a relinquishment of the physical pleasures of this world is worthwhile in the long run, and in truth, in the short run as well, as a life filled with meaning and purpose is well worth the sacrifice involved. Retrospectively, we will have given up nothing and will have gained eternity. It certainly is well worth a few extra dollars to arrive at one's destination with all of his luggage in hand.

It is always advisable to calculate the cost of a good deed against its reward, and the reward of a sin against its cost. This computation does not require a mathematical background in calculus and trigonometry. When one has a clear understanding that his true essence is his soul, then his perspective of true gain, or loss, is unequivocal. It rings clear that solely through the pursuit of emulating the ways of G-d will a person bring perfection to his true self. The temporary inconvenience of the effort required for this performance is miniscule. In contrast, the ephemeral pleasure of a sin is obscured by the regression it will bring to the soul and the damage to the true self. The calculation is simple, once we look with clear-sightedness at the big picture.

As one who has started many a diet, I can testify that the trick to success lies in getting past the first few days. Passing up the many sweets and delicacies, difficult as that may be, is well worth the unbelievable joy of finding a suit where not only does the jacket fit, but there is sufficient room in the waist so as not to endanger its wearer or subject him to the trial of the old switch-the-pants-in-the-dressing-room trick. The many health benefits of the successful dieter and exercise enthusiast, not only outweigh (no pun intended) any sacrifice involved, but render it insignificant, in light (no pun intended again) of the tremendous gain (okay, pun intended).

This is true for all important matters in life. The more significant it is, the more hard work is involved in its achievement. Olympic contenders endure years of training to reach the point of readiness for Olympic competition. No doubt it is all well worth the hundreds of wearisome hours of training when the gold medal is won. But it's more than that! The gold-medal winner would have had it no other way.

There is an event greater than the Olympics and its victories. There is a challenge that surpasses them all: the challenge of eternity, for which any and every sacrifice is worth its weight in gold. Retrospectively, the toil becomes part of the pleasure and enjoyment that enhances our lives in this temporary world, as we diligently prepare for an eternal existence.

We are all in Olympic competition. The flaming torch is ready to be passed. The preparation is rigorous and at times demands what may seem like disruptions of normative living and natural impulses. In truth, though, such toil only enriches our lives with meaning and purpose, with spirituality and holiness, with knowledge and wisdom, with an intimate relationship with our Creator. It is a life that is full and busy, with never a dull moment. It provides a life that allows us to shine and nourish our true selves in a way that ensures sustenance for eternity.

There is a Gold Medal awaiting us all, along with a spiritual euphoria that accompanies its acquisition, as we bask in the glory of the splendor of our Creator. The short-term sacrifice is long forgotten as we everlastingly relish the long-term gain.

OBLIVIOUS

Two elderly women were out for a Sunday drive in the old Lincoln Continental. Both could barely see over the dashboard. Cruising along, they came to an intersection. The light was red but they went straight through.

Sadie in the passenger seat thought to herself, "I must be losing it. I could have sworn we just went through a red light."

After a few minutes they came to another intersection where the light was red, and again they zipped right through it. This time, Sadie really was concerned that maybe her age had finally caught up with her, and she decided to pay very close attention at the next light.

Sure enough, at the next intersection the light was definitely red and they went right through. Sadie, now sure of herself, turned to her friend and said, "Mildred! Do you know we just ran three lights in a row? You could have killed us!"

Mildred turned to her and said, "Oh! Am I driving?"

ೞೞೞ

At times we live in absolute oblivion. We easily get lost in our thoughts, "spaced out" and in total "la-la land." Even when we are completely alert we would be foolish and naïve to think we know all that transpires around us.

We forget so quickly that we are mere mortals with limited vision and foresight. How many times have we driven our cars and changed lanes, lost in thought and unmindful of the rapidly approaching vehicle in the next lane, only to escape calamity by a fraction of a second? Unbeknownst to us there are internal and external events happening around us constantly that threaten our very existence, from which we miraculously escape harm. Unfortunately, we allow oblivion to germinate into atrophy of the senses and paralysis of the heart as we become apathetic and indifferent to the glory that surrounds us.

I am reminded of a true story of a man driving on the Palisades Parkway, a two-lane highway, listening to a lecture on his tape deck when he decided to change lanes. He signaled left and was about to move into the passing lane, oblivious to the large SUV passing him at 80 miles per hour. His move would have been catastrophic, had he not heard the honk of a horn coming from his right that instinctively caused him to veer back into his lane. Only then did he notice the speeding truck whiz by him, and he realized that he just been spared an almost certain fatal accident.

But when he looked to the right from where the sound of the honking horn had emanated, he saw no cars – only the forest. Only then did it dawn on him what had occurred. He had been listening to a lecture that had been given in an auditorium where the windows were open. Apparently a horn had honked in the street outside that auditorium and had wafted in through the windows, thus having been recorded on the tape that was sitting on the lecturer's lectern. At that precise moment when the man was about to change lanes he had heard that honk from his car's tape player, which is what had prompted him to turn back to safety.

Indeed some acquire their world with one turn. No doubt all of us acquire our world through the good graces of a power beyond us that watches and protects, sustains and nurtures, for which we are eternally grateful.

The Epitome of Balance and Symmetry

THE GREATEST SYMPHONY EVER WRITTEN — MANKIND.

The archangel inquires of G-d, "Where have you been, my Lord? We've been looking for you!"

With a deep sigh of satisfaction, G-d proudly points downward through the clouds and exclaims, "Look archangel! Look what I've made!"

"What is it?" the angel asks.

"It's a planet!" replies G-d. "And I've put life on it. I'm going to call it Earth. It's going to be a place of great balance."

"Balance?" asks the angel still confused.

"For example," G-d continues, pointing to the different parts of the earth. "Northern Europe will be a place of great opportunity and wealth, while southern Europe will be ravaged with intense poverty. Over there I've established a continent filled with natural resources, while there a continent replete with desert. That one over there will be extremely hot, while that one to the north will be frigid and cold."

The angel, impressed by G-d's handiwork, then points to a particular area and says, "What's that over there?"

"Ah, that?" says G-d. "That's Washington state, the most glorious place on the Earth. There are beautiful mountains, rivers, and streams, lakes, forests, hills, plains, caverns, and underground creeks. The people from there will be handsome, modest, intelligent, and humorous. They will be found traveling the world, respected by all. They will be extremely sociable, charismatic, hardworking, high achieving, universally renowned as diplomats and emissaries of peace."

The archangel gasps in admiration, but then the thought occurs to him:

"But G-d, what about the balance You promised? You said there would be balance!"

G-d smiles and says, "Don't you worry! There is another Washington... Wait until you see the fools I put there!"

⋘⋙

We all stand in awe of G-d's incredible creation. The symphony of the universe is mind-boggling and overwhelmingly impressive. The symmetry and balance of the cosmos, the amazing blend and equilibrium of the forces of creation, the homeostasis and wondrous miracle of the human function, all leave us goggle-eyed and openmouthed. Indeed, we live in an extraordinary world. From Niagara Falls to the Grand Canyon, from the Alps to the Himalayas and everything in between, we are humbled by the magnificence of G-d's deeds and the profundity of His thoughts, albeit confined by our limited capacity to comprehend the superhuman events that surround us.

Were we to clearly perceive the fundamental interaction of the flow of the creation, were we to properly appreciate the millions of nuances of its divinely inspired instrumentation, were we capable of comprehending this massive implementation – we would shudder in trepidation of the Master of the Universe and marvel at His glorious world.

Yet the greatest demonstration of this balance and symmetry in Creation is in man himself. Adam, the first man, was created as a composite of all that existed, as G-d's mandate to create Adam was addressed to the entire Creation, with all contributing an aspect of man's essence. As descendants of Adam, mankind has the great task of juggling and balancing itself in order to generate an equilibrium that will find favor in the eyes of G-d and in the eyes of man. As we ascend and prevail from victory to victory in our pursuit of perfection, we elevate the world along with ourselves, bringing ourselves and our surroundings closer to perfection. That harmonious blend of greatness and humility, of control and balance, of body and soul, of emulating the ways of the Master Conductor, is a symphony that has no rival, a sonata that has no equal.

Unfortunately, one rarely sees man acting as the noble being that he could be. Instead of symmetry, there is chaos; instead of concordance, there is bedlam; instead of congruity, there is confusion. Instead of emulating G-d's attributes, there is greed and envy, haughtiness and egoism, anger and pettiness. In the place of balance there is instability, as man remains the "unfinished symphony" – or worse, the never developed one. As the true dimensions of man wither away, the perfect man becomes a rarity, an endangered species.

Nonetheless, those of us who have enjoyed the privilege of observing saintliness and seeing greatness understand that mankind can still shine in its full glory. Those who have read the many available biographies of the righteous and the upright can affirm their belief in man's potential for perfection no matter how puny and pathetic, shriveled and shrunken the reality of humankind has become in the world at large.

We will not succumb to the mindless complacency and soulless acceptance of the frailty and feebleness of man that has become endemic. We are energized by the saintly men and women both contemporary and of times past. We are inspired by the symphony of their worlds and the completeness of their lives. We still believe with complete faith that man can strive for perfection, that he can actualize his innate spiritual abilities to their fullest. And in his doing so, the most majestic sunset will pale in comparison to the astonishing brilliance of the complete man that he will have become.

What's in a Name?

A GOOD NAME IS THE GREATEST COMMODITY.

The charming and dashing presidential candidate confidently entered the nursing home with his entourage and approached an elderly lady sitting in a wheelchair.

"Good morning, ma'am! How are you today?"

The old lady didn't give him the time of day.

"Ma'am, do you know who I am? Do you know my name?" the seasoned politician pressed.

Again, the old lady all but ignored him.

Speaking a little louder this time, he said, "Ma'am, are you sure you don't recognize me? Don't you know my name?"

"No, I don't know your name," she replied, "but if you go to the front desk, I'm sure they can help you figure it out!"

છ૭જ૭ક૭ન૭

A person's name is his identity and becomes the symbol by which his individual characteristics and personality are distinguished and known. The mere mention of this appellation conjures up an entire history of that person's life and accomplishments. Often one's name is a link in a chain to previous generations and a perpetuation of those no longer here. Most assuredly, it is a representation of one's persona and image.

A nickname could brand a person for life and negatively impact on his self-confidence. Sticks and stones do break bones and names can indeed break people. It is said by some that a name may even be an indicator of what can be expected from a person in the future, a prophetic manifestation of his or her being. However, no matter what a person's name may be, the most important thing to remember are the words of King Solomon that "a good name is better than good oil."

What is a "good name"? How does one attain it?

A "good name" is a person's reputation. It is his pleasant interaction with others, his kindness and good deeds. It is his stepping out of the box and developing sensitivity for others, free of the self-oriented incarceration that often grips man. It is his "good morning" greeting and his smile, his "please" and his "thank you." It is his general appreciation and demonstration of that appreciation to others for what he receives from them, for which he is eternally grateful. It is his ability to focus on giving, not taking, with sincere empathy and outright generosity. It is his meticulous honesty and integrity in word and in deed, and natural inclination to cleave to truth and run far away from all that is false. It is his contagious positive attitude and upbeat personality, never slandering others, that impacts others to act the same. It is his sincere humility and his inability to take credit for the G-d-given gift of life. The mention of his name evokes a response of, "What a prince of a person, a perfect gentleman, a woman of valor, absolute nobility and aristocracy!"

BETWEEN Man and His Fellow Man

A Small Step for Man, a Giant Step for Mankind

STRIVE TO BE CONSIDERATE AND NEVER TAKE ADVANTAGE.

Miss Jones had been giving her second-grade students a lesson on science. She had explained the mechanism of magnets and demonstrated how they would pick up nails and other bits of iron. The children were markedly impressed.

Now it was question time. Miss Jones wanted to see if the students had properly absorbed the lesson, and she asked: "Tell me who I am. My name begins with an 'm' and I pick up things. What am I?"

Little Johnny in the front row proudly exclaimed, "You're a mother!"

಩ఇఇ಑ఇఇ

Our mothers have been good to us, perhaps too good. They have acted as our personal valet, our cleaning lady, and even, at times, our slave. They have cooked for us, often specifically for us, because we didn't like anything else. They have made our favorite desserts and have done countless acts of kindness and self-sacrifice on our behalf. However, their little "baby" could potentially develop into a big "baby" and take his "slave mentality" (that others are his slaves) into his marriage. The "M" for "mother" can easily be inverted into a "W" for "wife," and the spoiled child could become a demanding husband, who expects much and gives little in return.

As much as our mothers and wives derive great pleasure in catering to our every need, we would be remiss were we to take undue advantage of their graciousness. To carelessly throw our clothing around the room for our mothers and wives to pick up, to leave our plates and other paraphernalia on the table without concern of the mess we've left behind, and for that matter to leave the crumpled piece of paper on the floor near the wastepaper basket – another missed shot from the next LeBron James – is a major "disconnect" in the growth process of an aspiring "giver." On the other hand, when we lend a hand and make that modest gesture that says "I appreciate your hard work," when we show that we don't take anyone or anything for granted, then we've taken a gigantic leap, with just a small step, that has eternal value.

I'll never forget one of the rules in the rabbinical college I attended, where classes began at 9:00 a.m., that anyone who didn't make his bed in his dormitory room was to be called out of class to attend to his duties. Naturally, there were those who deliberately left their beds unmade. A note was brought into the classroom by one of the workers smack in the middle of the lecture, with a list of the names of the culprits. The eternal message of the school administration that good manners are fundamental to intellectual pursuit was very clear.

One of the sweetest recollections I have of my father, of blessed memory, is the memory of him standing with a towel wrapped around his waist as an apron as he washed the dishes, unsolicited by my mother. It was certainly not beneath his dignity. In my mind, as a small child, it only enhanced his dignity.

The well-known story about a great rabbi and a young aspiring scholar comes to mind. Although I've been told by some that the story may not be authentic, it serves the point well. It seems that this newly married member of the graduate program of the rabbinical college went to the dean to inquire if it was proper for his wife to ask him, a budding scholar, to take out the garbage. The dean seemed to understand this young man's concerns, and the young man left, under the impression that his mentor had acquiesced to his side in the young couple's altercation.

The next morning at 7:00 a.m. the doorbell rang at the home of this young graduate student, who, upon opening the door, was startled to see the esteemed rabbi standing on his threshold.

"Good morning! Is everything all right? What brings the rabbi here so early in the morning?" the young man asked.

"I came to take out the garbage," the rabbi responded. "Somebody has to take out the garbage!" Needless to say, the young man learned a lesson of a lifetime.

Emissaries of G-d

GIVING CHARITY MEANS GETTING MORE THAN YOU GIVE.

Early one morning, the president surreptitiously slipped out of the White House for his daily jog without the accompaniment of the Secret Service. Suddenly, a man wearing a ski mask jumped out from behind some bushes with a gun in his hand and screamed out, "Give me all of your money!"

Unwilling to relinquish his cash, the president replied, "You can't do this! Do you know who I am? Why, I'm the president of the United States of America!"

"Oh!" the thief responded. "Strike that then. Give me all of my money."

છ ભ ૭ ૪

Whose money is it anyway? Truth be told, it's neither mine nor yours, but G-d's. We are merely His agents, entrusted to carry out the proper transactions. Indeed, "charity begins at home" – that is, it originates at the home base, the throne of the Master of the Universe.

In the recent investment scandal of 2008–2009, in which so many people absorbed major fiscal losses, a man went to his mentor, a great sage, lamenting his massive loss of one million dollars to this notorious scheme. Instead of the consolation he expected, the wise man's response was pure and simple: "Do you mean to say that you had a million dollars in your hands and you held on to it, instead of disbursing it among the many various worthy charities in need? Remember, my dear son, that we are merely envoys of G-d, emissaries, acting in good faith, to help distribute the necessary funds."

The tragic events of the 9/11 attack on the World Trade Center and the subsequent financial losses, as well as the more recent crash of global markets and the plunge of the universal trust of 2008, are ample indications that we are being sent a clear message: a reassessment of our financial affixation and preoccupation is in order.

The well-known adage of the wisest of all men, King Solomon, "Charity protects one from death," is not only significant because the great merit that an individual earns through his or her charity provides heavenly protection from dying, but is to be understood on a practical level as well. If a person takes upon himself to act as Heaven's agent in distributing His funds, then longevity is his, simply because he is an essential part of the program. As one of G-d's trustees, his position in life is secured in the legal domain of "an agent acts in the place of his sender." In this case he acts as an agent of the Source of all life and thereby inevitably draws vivacity and effervescence from his dispatcher – G-d Himself. Indeed his services are welcomed for many years to come as he works hand in hand with his Creator, securing his lifeline, here and eternally.

Everybody Counts
(I Don't Get No Respect)

HONOR EACH PERSON BY FOCUSING ON THEIR POTENTIAL FOR GREATNESS.

A well-known funnyman once lamented: "When I was young I didn't get no respect. One winter, I asked my father if I could go ice-skating on the frozen pond.

"He said, 'Son, why don't you wait until the weather warms up?'"

⌘⌘⌘⌘

Everyone needs respect. The alternative is catastrophic. Whether it is a child, an adult, a student, a teacher, a boss, an employee, a coworker, a husband, a wife, a grandparent, or a friend, the need to feel and to know that others respect your existence is as essential as the air you breathe. To be looked at as a number is an unfortunate consequence of our bureaucracy and grossly detracts from a person's singularity, uniqueness, and special inner strength.

As much as respect and honor from others is crucial to man's survival in life, the pursuit of it could mark his ruin. Uncontrolled desire for honor will preoccupy his every thought and control his life. He will never be satisfied with the honor he receives, always deeming it insufficient for a man of his importance. His mindset will be such that even when he isn't actively engaged in pursuing honor, he will be looking over his shoulder constantly to see if it is following him. To get "no respect" is indeed damaging; to be preoccupied with receiving it is debilitating and consuming.

The proper balance must be struck, where one gives honor and respect to others anticipating nothing in return. Then the honor will indeed pursue him, for he will be properly deserving of it and be capable of receiving it in a healthy manner.

In order to focus on showering others with respect, a person needs to recognize each individual's potential for greatness. Respect is not exclusively for those who have already accrued massive accomplishments in life, but applies to every member of the human race. All of mankind was created in the image of G-d and thereby is destined for greatness, if only we will unlock and tap into our unique strengths and talents. We honor people because they are worthy of honor, as they are the epitome of G-d's creation and have the greatest likeness to Him. They are thinking and articulate, sensitive and caring, broad and expansive, and capable of life-giving contributions to others with whom they interact in the course of their lives. They deserve our utmost respect, and when we accord them that honor, they will in turn honor us. We will live in harmony together on this earth, mutually respectful, our confidence boosted, and our potential for achievement greatly enhanced.

Giving, Never Taking

"A GOOD MORNING, A GOOD YEAR" — GIVING MORE THAN YOU GET.

A man parked his new Bentley outside of a prestigious Midtown Manhattan bank and rushed in to see a bank official about a loan. "I'd like to borrow $50,000 as soon as possible," he requested.

"Do you realize that in addition to your responsibility for the loan itself, you will be assuming the repayment of the interest at a high rate for the five years of the terms of this loan, should it be approved?" the clerk inquired.

"Yes! Absolutely!" the man responded

"Do you have something you can put down as collateral against the loan?" the bank clerk requested.

"Sure thing!" said the man. "That's my Bentley parked outside. Here are the keys. Take them!"

"Fine, here is your bank check for $50,000," said the clerk. He ordered the security guard to park the car in the bank's underground lot and the man was on his way.

Just a week later, the man was back with the $50,000 cash plus the interest payment, to the bank clerk's utter surprise. "If you had the money all along, why did you bother taking out the loan in the first place?" he asked.

Handing over the $50,000 debt plus the twenty-five dollars in accumulated interest the man responded, "Are you kidding? Where else can you get a week's underground parking in Midtown Manhattan for only twenty-five bucks!"

We have become a society of takers and manipulators. The better one maneuvers, the more he advances. Our approach to life has become one of "what's in it for me?" The days of "ask not what your country can do for you, but what you can do for your country," have been replaced with stimulus packages and bailouts. Our behavior is a far cry from people of yesteryear, who were hesitant to gain benefit from others at all, and held onto a conduct of self-reliance so as not to develop the character trait of a "taker," whether or not it was at someone else's expense.

Instead, we have become a "give me" generation in which we think everything is coming to us. We must somehow get a handle on things so that we don't succumb to this self-serving, "swipe the plastic" attitude that reflects the "give me" posture of society at large.

There were people not so long ago who had the ingrained custom to respond to the greeting "Good morning" with "Good morning, a good year." Their motive was to ensure that they always gave back more than they received, that they evolve into a giver and not a taker. You were kind enough to wish me a good day; I therefore want to not only wish you a good day in return, but to add on to what you've given me by wishing you a blessing for a good year. (Of course this could go on forever!)

There is holiness and purity in giving. In doing so one emulates the Creator, Who is constantly giving. The Talmud speaks of a great rabbi who made a living as a shoemaker. When he would construct a shoe, he would make it with the calculated intention that it be a strong shoe, a durable shoe, one that would serve its wearer well for many years. His focus, even in the course of his business, was to give, and thereby he converted a mundane act into one infused with holiness.

Compare such thinking with the "take as much as you can get" attitude of today's "make it to break it and discard" manufacturers, and one understands that the impurity has spread way beyond the confines of promiscuity and licentiousness. The self-centeredness of the "taker" is sure to lead to the fragmentation that is at the core of all that is impure, for the greater the abandonment of the character traits of the Source of all life – the "Supreme Giver" – the greater that impurity will be.

Happy With "His" Portion

Two Irish fellows are walking their dogs one day when they come upon a pub. Finding it difficult not to imbibe, one says to the other, "How about stopping in for a drink?"

The other replies, "We can't go in there like this! Don't you see the sign? 'Absolutely no pets allowed!'"

Undeterred, the first guy adjusts his sunglasses as he and his German shepherd head toward the tavern door.

"Hey! You can't go in there with that dog! Can't you see the sign?" screams the burly bouncer.

"But I'm blind," the man replies, "and this is my seeing-eye dog!"

"I am so sorry!" the bouncer apologizes profusely. "Please go right in and have a drink on the house."

His friend, having observed this, tries the same routine. After adjusting his sunglasses, he approaches the tavern door with his dog, only to be stopped by the bouncer. "Hey, you! You can't go in there with a dog! Can't you see the sign?" the bouncer screams out again.

"But I'm blind," the man replies, "and this is my seeing-eye dog."

"You call this a seeing-eye dog?" questions the bouncer. "A Chihuahua?"

"Oh," says the "blind" man. "Is that what they gave me?"

છ૦ગ૪૭ઠ

All too often, we focus on what everyone else has and what we lack, instead of appreciating and treasuring our G-d-given uniqueness and purpose. In our nonsensical yearning to be someone else, we lose sight of what we were given, and our singular task on this earth.

It gets worse than that. At times, we can get so caught up and enamored with the other person's world, his talents and successes, his celebrations and family dynamics, his scholarship and erudition, that we squander our world in the process. All we have in the end is the pain of envy and the anguish of disappointment. But, it's even worse than that.

The Talmud shares with us the proverbial saying: "The camel went to seek horns for himself. Not only did he not procure horns, his ears were cut off as well." The envious person risks losing his own distinctiveness in the process of his envy, and that is the saddest part of all. He will thereby never actualize the potential that was uniquely and only his, never to accomplish those things that nobody else in the world could touch but him. And instead of coming in contact with his soul's calling and concretizing his vast potential; instead of standing up to the challenges that are unambiguously his, and only his, to hurdle, he surrenders his entire raison d'être for a tradeoff of futility. He will never touch that which was designated for his friend, and he will lose all that was uniquely his own, for whoever focuses on that which is not his – what he seeks, he never gets, and what he has, is taken away from him.

The one who is truly happy with his lot will, in fact, be both thrilled with his lot and his friend's lot. He will be ecstatic about his special and personal contribution to the world during the course of his human experience and equally exhilarated that his friend, with his own unique portion, has the opportunity to accomplish the same in a way that only he can. Happiness only eludes us because we lose our focus, because we choose to live vicariously through others instead of capitalizing on all the gifts that are uniquely ours. We are replete with an abundance of distinctive potential that is capable of building worlds. There is much to look forward to; there is much reason to rejoice.

Invisible

THE SILENT TREATMENT CAN BE DESTRUCTIVE.

The nurse barged into the doctor's office. "Doctor, Doctor! You must come immediately! There's a man outside who thinks he's invisible!"

The doctor turned to the nurse and said, "Tell him I can't see him right now!"

How often have we walked into a new environment or a strange setting and have felt invisible? No one said hello, nobody even gestured a hint of recognition that there was a new face in the crowd. Physically, we knew we existed, but it was as if we were transparent to everyone else in the room. Somehow we faded into oblivion without even trying, simply because we were not from that town. We lost our identity before we even had a chance to identify ourselves. We felt weightless as if we had no presence. This silent treatment is a display of humiliation that didn't have to be. Ignorance may be bliss, but being ignored is painful and hurtful. All of this could have been averted with a few simple words: "Good morning. Are you new in town?" A warm greeting, a sensitive word, a welcoming smile, all send a clear message: "You do exist! I recognize your presence! You are not invisible!"

This is not simply a matter of hospitality or good manners. Our greeting one another is a barometer of the extent to which we respect and value another human being. If I can pass you by and not feel your presence, then I relegate you to an inanimate object that has no feelings. On the other hand, when I greet you warmly, I give life and rejuvenate your existence.

Historically, the severity of not showing proper respect to other human beings has been hard-hitting and catastrophic. From segregation to pogroms, from inequality to holocausts and genocide, such atrocity finds its origin in a general lack of respect. Needless to say, this insensitivity and the degradation that follows come in different flavors and stripes, varied levels and realms, but the common thread among all instances of it is a preoccupation with one's self, which incapacitates one to see and respect his friend for the noble and prestigious human being that he is. That being the case, he views his fellow man as one who has very little to offer him, to the point that he is no more than a disappearing shadow, a mirage at best. I might have greeted him, but I didn't see anyone there. He really was invisible. I made sure of it!

Kindness without an Agenda

Carol's parents were not too thrilled with her new companion. It was bad enough that she was only sixteen and he was twenty, but in addition to that, his appearance was frightening. His hair was long and styled in dreadlocks; he had tattoos all over his arms and piercings in both his ears and nose. It didn't help that his leather jacket was etched with skulls and bones, interlaced with the design of a machete and a switchblade.

Trying to be as diplomatic as possible, they appealed to their daughter. "Carol, he just doesn't look particularly kind!"

"What?" Carol responded. "Not kind? You must be kidding! If he wasn't kind, would he be doing forty hours a week of community service?"

ശ൞ഐൌ

The true meaning of kindness often eludes us. The master of kindness is one who is able to cross the line that divides between living a life that is self-serving and doing for others without any personal gain. When a person is able to get past the point that marks the difference between the requisite and that which is not strictly necessary, when he has developed a deeper understanding of what it means to emulate the ways of G-d that transcends all minimal requirements, he has entered the world of true benevolence.

The literature describes the kindness shown to the deceased as "kindness of truth," indicative of selfless involvement in the needs of others without any expectations of a remuneration (dead people don't return favors). Such kindness mimics the kindness of our Creator and is on a level all by itself.

Unfortunately, at times our idea of kindness is wrapped up in how much we receive in return. A charity donation can become subordinate to how much honor it will bring; hospitality, to what degree can these guests entertain me; matchmaking, to whether I can add another couple to my list of successes; and even volunteer services, to what degree can I act as a "big shot" and command respect. And although most people are sincere and well-meaning in their humanitarian efforts, it is still difficult for one to be totally selfless, even as he gives to others.

A great sage related the well-known parable of the man who loves fish. A well-dressed man entered a restaurant and placed his order. "Oh! You have fish on the menu? Why, I love fish! I just love it! Give me the fish," he tells the waiter. A naive fellow sitting nearby overhears the man's order, and he foolishly believes that the waiter will bring out some fish in a bowl of water and the man who loves fish will tickle the fish and play with them. After all, "he loves fish!" Instead, to his utter astonishment, he watches the waiter bring out a steaming platter of broiled salmon. Then, to his further shock and dismay, he sees the man pick up his knife and fork, stab the poor, dead fish, and begin eating it. Appalled that the man could act so harshly to the fish that he supposedly loves, he approaches him with sharp rebuke: "You love fish? You don't love fish! You love yourself!"

Our love of kindness must be unadulterated and pure. It must be a true love of kindness and not a love of oneself. We must love it and do it for no ulterior motive, but rather simply because we are trying to emulate our Creator, Who built an entire world out of kindness, and we endeavor to mimic and imitate His every move.

Selflessness

A woman calls Mt. Sinai Hospital. "Hello, I'd like to talk to you about a certain patient's condition. Please give me a full report, not just if she's 'stable' or 'critical.' I want to know the details from top to bottom, from A to Z."

"That's somewhat of an unusual request," says the operator. "I'll have to connect you to a supervisor."

An authoritative voice comes on the line. "Yes? How can I help you?"

"I'm calling about Rose Frankel in room 302. Can you please fill me in on her condition, in detail?"

"Let me see...Farber, Finkel, Frankel. Yes, here it is, Rose Frankel. She's off oxygen, she finished her antibiotics, the feeding tube is out, she's eaten three square meals, and she looks quite alert. As a matter of fact the doctor says that if she keeps improving, he's going to send her home on Tuesday."

The woman on the other end is ecstatic. "Oh! Thank G-d! That's wonderful! That's great news! I am so happy to hear that! She's going home already on Tuesday! That's marvelous!"

The supervisor responds, "Ma'am, from your genuine concern and enthusiasm, I take it you must be a very dear friend or close relative?"

"What friend or relative?" the woman says. "This is Rose Frankel!! My doctor, he doesn't tell me anything!"

To be concerned about others as much as we are concerned about ourselves would be quite an achievement. To be sensitive to another at one's own expense is an even greater accomplishment. When it involves giving up what one justly deserves in favor of another, it is an act of outstanding piety that is worthy of praise. It is, in a sense, giving one's life to another in the most selfless fashion.

Such was the selflessness of Rachel, the future matriarch of Israel. Out of concern that Laban, her dishonest father, would clandestinely "pull some type of trick" and sneak her older sister Leah under the wedding canopy in her place, she and her husband-to-be, Jacob, had arranged certain "signs" between them to evade his chicanery. However, at the last moment, concerned about her sister's possible embarrassment, Rachel gave away those special signs to her sister, signs that would have exposed her father Laban's deception. Not only did she relinquish her husband-to-be and potentially her future as a matriarch of the Jewish people, not only did she absorb the embarrassment of not being the bride at her own wedding and risked incurring the wrath of a disappointed groom, but she even lowered herself to hide under the bed in the course of an intimacy, which rightfully was hers, so she could respond to Jacob's call – all so that Leah's voice would not be detected.

It is this self-sacrifice that stands at the core of Rachel's ongoing prayer and cry that her children return from their painful exile. It is this altruism that makes her prayers so penetrating, even posthumously; for until this very day, thousands flock to Rachel's Tomb to pray that Rachel continue to intercede on behalf of her children by virtue of the eternal merit of her epic self-sacrifice.

The unflinching love between David and Jonathan, described by King David as he laments his devoted friend's demise as "more wondrous than the love of women," metaphorically is a reference to two famous women, Rachel and Leah. That Jonathan, the son of King Saul, could be so relinquishing to abdicate the crown that would have been his to his best friend – without a trace of envy, and with absolute determination to become his trusted servant

– was a bequest from the love of those particular women, Rachel to Leah. Rachel had infused selflessness into the bloodstream of her descendants (Jonathan was from the tribe of Benjamin, Rachel's son), enabling Jonathan to rise to the occasion.

Life offers a multiplicity of opportunities to be relinquishing and forgiving, instead of harsh and vengeful. When we respond to the various situations in which we have been wronged with selflessness and self-sacrifice, we should know that, difficult as it may be, we have achieved a level of greatness on those occasions that is priceless and enduring eternally.

Sharing and Caring

SPREAD YOUR BLANKET OVER OTHERS!

A young man, standing in line behind an elderly couple at McDonalds, couldn't help from overhearing their frugal order of just one serving of a burger and fries, with one soft drink, and two cups.

The elderly husband proceeded to the table with his tray, where he carefully divided the hamburger in two equal parts, and tenderly placed half of it before his wife. He then meticulously counted out the french fries: one for him, and one for her, one for him, and one for her, until each of them had the same amount. Afterwards, he measured half of the soft drink into the extra cup and set it in front of his wife, leaving the other half for himself. The old man then began to eat, but his wife just sat there watching him, with her hands folded on her lap.

The young man's compassion was aroused. He approached their table and politely requested that he be allowed to purchase another meal for them, at his expense.

"Absolutely not!" said the husband. "We've been married for fifty years and everything has always been shared 50/50, and always will be shared 50/50! That's how it has always been, and that's how it will continue to be, forever!" The old man sat down and continued to eat his meager portion as his wife just sat and watched, her hands folded on her lap.

The young man couldn't take it anymore and turned to the elderly wife, who still sat there passively, and asked, "Excuse me, ma'am, but aren't you going to eat?"

The old lady smiled and replied, "Oh, not yet! It's his turn to use the teeth!"

The Talmud describes the greatest generation of Torah study as one that was so destitute that six students had to share one blanket. Despite the tremendous erudition of other generations, this impoverished generation eclipsed them all. Was it simply that they persevered in their learning in spite of their dire straits, or was there more to it?

A great rabbi suggested that this distinction was based upon the character of these worthy students. It is one thing to share a blanket with five others, and quite another to ensure that the others are properly covered and warm. The novelty of that generation was that six were covered with one blanket and, in fact, all were covered. Their sharing was one of absolute caring, as they were able to step outside of themselves, and place the warmth and comfort of the next person before their own comfort. Their wisdom was preceded by, and predicated on, fear of Heaven. It wasn't about them or their success in learning, as much as it was about serving their Creator. Their egos were incapacitated by their fear of G-d, and replaced with a spirit of mutuality and reciprocity, built upon respect for mankind and humility before G-d.

In a meeting with the CEOs from some major American companies, all secular Jews, the dean of one of the world's largest rabbinical academies in Israel asked them what they thought to be the most significant lesson of the Holocaust. Some of them responded with "We will never forget!" Others suggested that "We will never again allow ourselves to be bystanders to such evil."

The venerable rabbi begged to differ. "The greatest lesson of the Holocaust," he explained, "is about the essence of the human spirit of a Jewish soul. With Jews killed outright or beaten to a pulp and left to die; with others crammed into cattle cars to travel for days without food and water; with indescribable selections and heart-wrenching separations from their loved ones, which were usually forever; with those who survived shoved into overcrowded barracks of inhumane proportions – one would expect the one in every six inmates issued a blanket to keep the skimpy cover for himself. Yet that was the defining moment where the spirit of mankind shone forth with brilliance, for every man was sure to spread his blanket over five of his brothers.

"My friends," he concluded, "go back to America and spread your blankets over five others."

That's His Problem

Harry was a chronic worrier. He was always tense and nervous. Nothing could calm his incessant neurosis. His friends knew him as "Harry the Worrier."

One day, Harry's friends noticed a dramatic change in him. He was relaxed and laid-back, without a care in the world.

"Harry! What's happened to you? You look great. You're like a new person!"

"Well," said Harry, "I don't worry anymore. I hired a professional worrier to worry for me. I pay him $1,000 a week and I haven't had a single concern since."

"Harry! $1,000 a week? How can you to afford to pay him?" his friends asked.

"Pay him?" asked Harry. "That's his problem!"

附略

How many times do we shirk our responsibility to the needs of the community by saying: "Oh, that's someone else's problem. I need not concern myself with it"? Were everyone to rationalize this way, nothing would ever be accomplished.

We are thankful for those courageous few who assume responsibility and sacrifice themselves to the needs of others in their midst. Self-sacrifice is not easy, whether for the community or for strangers. To give without receiving in return demands an altruism that is replete with humility. To be involved on that level requires selflessness and self-sacrifice with little appreciation in return. Instead, one must tolerate much criticism and many complaints. Everyone knows better, yet each has an excuse why he can't get involved. The brave soul who does get involved sheds all semblance of self and focuses on the cause and the need.

Even if on paper it makes no sense, and a person doesn't have the time, the energy, or the resources, nonetheless, with willpower and a strong belief that those who assume responsibility will be given the strength and the means, such a person will meet with success. The many volunteer firefighters and ambulance personnel, the dedicated founders of charities and social organizations, laymen who assume the civic and religious burdens of their respective communities are living proof that where there is a will there is a way, especially when it involves one person giving of him- or herself for the sake of the many.

It takes a certain "leap of faith" to put oneself out in this fashion. Altruistic people must trust that one day they will be rewarded for all of their devotion. Meanwhile, they are happy to continue their "giving" for the many worthy causes because their immediate reward is the satisfaction they feel in escaping the confines of a limited and self-oriented existence to one that is free and expansive, where indeed someone else's problem is their own.

Trust You? Why, I Don't Even Know You!

BUILDING TRUST IN A WORLD SATURATED WITH GREED.

A man was approached by a mugger in Brooklyn and had no money in his pocket. Petrified that he might be physically attacked by his assailant, he took out his checkbook and nervously said, "L-L-Let me write you out a check!"

"A check? I should take a check from you? I should trust you with a check?" the mugger screamed at him. "WHY, I DON'T EVEN KNOW YOU!"

ෆ๛ඁ෭

In the unraveling of society, its mores and standards, people have lost the mutual trust that once was a given. In recent years, with the fall of the economy and the bankruptcy of so many "worthy" institutions in whom people had placed their trust, not to mention their life savings, consumer confidence has sunk to an all-time low. Personal greed and money hoarding has become public knowledge, leaving a trail of unfortunate victims behind. Politicians of both parties have used their position to benefit themselves at the expense of their very constituency. Credit markets are hesitant to lend, investors reluctant to endow, creating a flip-flop, topsy-turvy, here today–gone tomorrow, unpredictable global meltdown that has the whole world shaking. It all boils down to one thing: a worldwide lack of trust.

Because we have endured many a disappointment in the decadent behavior of mankind, we easily lose faith in the human experience. And although we would, nonetheless, like to believe that there still exists some semblance of decency and integrity in this world, as time goes on, one thing or another diminishes that dream. The fiscal fallout and stock market crash of the fall of 2008 have wreaked havoc on our reliance on our fellow man, and have weakened man's resolve to work harmoniously in the spirit of "everybody gains and nobody loses."

Yet we know that man cannot live without mutual trust. Businesses cannot thrive, nor can the crucial interpersonal relationships of life survive in a climate of dishonesty and infidelity. The decline of marriage as an institution, the unwillingness of so many to make that commitment, and the utter demise of the family unit in its wake are examples of the major casualties of a society bereft of trust.

Where do we begin? Trust is built with an absolute adherence to all that is true and an unequivocal abhorrence for that which is false. A "white lie" can be the beginning of a "big lie," and is soon followed by disloyalty and fraud. There is nothing more praiseworthy than one who is meticulous in his integrity in a world saturated with greed and cupidity. Let us endeavor to be counted among that select few and help rebuild our trust and faith in mankind.

We'll Leave the Light On for You

A man walks into the office of a cardiologist and says, "Excuse me, Doctor, I have a big problem. I think I am a moth."

The doctor berates him, "Listen! I'm a busy man. I'm not a psychiatrist, I'm a cardiologist. I'm sure you saw the sign on the door. Why did you come in here in the first place?"

"Oh! I don't know," the man says. "I guess I saw the light on, so I came right in!"

❦

In the darkness of this world, which prevails so heavily upon us today, people are eager to find a little "light," warmth, and encouragement to get them through their day. Motel 6 knows quite well how attractive their slogan, "We'll leave the light on for you," is to the lonely traveler on the dark highway. And, indeed, all of us, traversing the complex paths of life, are in need of the support and security of something bright and gleaming.

There are those who suffer from a psycho-physiological disorder in which their moods are affected by the lack of sunlight. For these people, winters are horrific and despondency dominates. In truth, whose mood is not vastly improved by a sunny day or by a change from cold winter weather to a milder climate? So many people migrate to Florida or California to spend their winter break in a more welcoming atmosphere.

But there is a simpler way to bring sunshine to the world and lift up the spirits of those in our environs. It is a talent every person possesses: the ability to smile. A smile nourishes. It acts as sunshine does to a plant. A good word, a compliment, a bit of encouragement, a pat on the back, a warm greeting, putting forth the effort to remember someone's name or situation – all of these simple acts of kindness give the other person a much-needed boost of energy and infuse him or her with nourishment and nutrition.

Life can be very lonely at times. We need to know that there are others who are thinking of us; that there are people who care and are concerned about our lives, who will help light up our day and brighten our perspective. Indeed such empathy will assuage our burden and lift up our spirits. Let us endeavor to be that source of energy to others and most certainly one smile will breed another, and we too will be revitalized in the process.

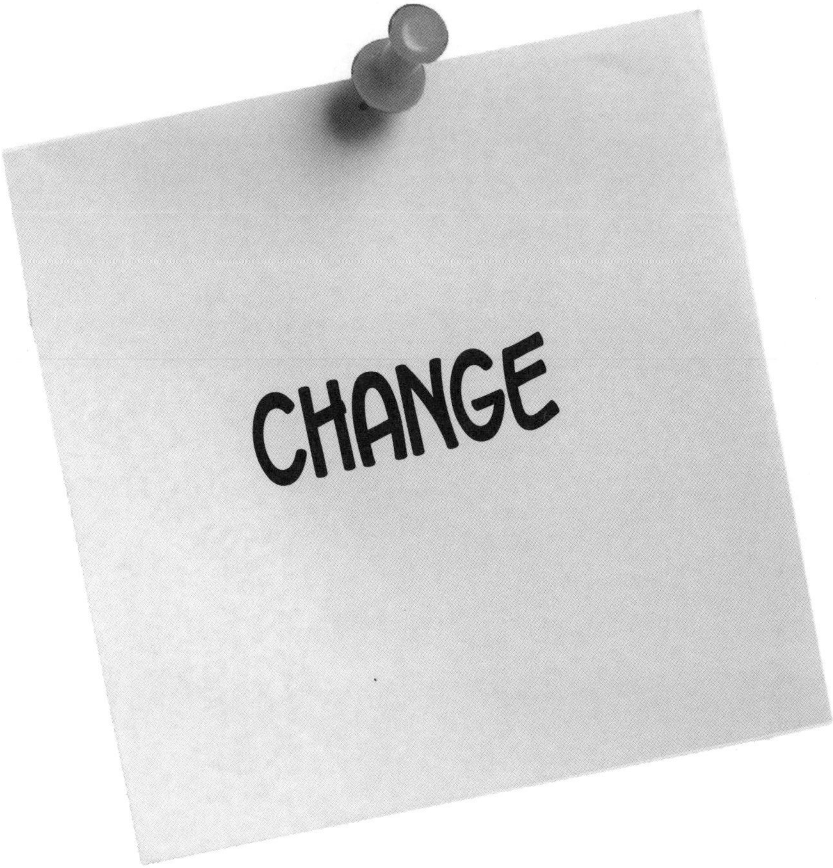
CHANGE

A Change of Heart

CHANGE IS POSSIBLE – IT'S JUST A TURN AWAY.

Fernando was well known as a house painter for the wealthy. He had made his fortune painting the palatial homes of the rich and the famous. Upon his retirement, as he was about to impart the secret of his success to his son, Bernardo, he said the following:

"Son, I want you to know that I started out like any other house painter, scratching around for any job I could get."

"So how did you become so well known and popular among the affluent people, Papa?" asked Bernardo.

"There was this extremely wealthy woman from Scarsdale who collected antiques. Her prime acquisition was an ancient lamp that she kept on the night table in her bedroom, which she cherished, absolutely enthralled with its color. She sought out a painter who could match the color of the room to the color of the lamp. Painters came and went, but nobody could satisfy her keen eye for pigment and hue. I applied as well, and she hired me. Pleased with my work, she recommended me to all her fancy friends, and the rest is history."

"But, Papa, how were you able to succeed in matching the walls of the room to the color of the lamp, when all those others failed?" asked Bernardo.

"My dear son! I never changed the color of the wall. I changed the color of the lamp!"

Change is difficult, and at times it seems impossible. The power of habit takes its toll on the human psyche, convincing us that there can be no other path but the one we have taken. We become victims of our past failures to alter our behavior, and then succumb to the malaise of complacency and mediocrity. In an advertisement to encourage people to switch their telephone service, a billboard proclaimed: "If you think you can never change, think back to how you wore your hair for your high school graduation picture." (We men might find it hard to imagine a time when we even had hair!)

Everyone can change! As a matter of fact, change is inevitable (except from vending machines), but we need to use all of our skill and insight to systematically plot out and plan our strategy, in order for this metamorphosis to be successful and enduring.

Unfortunately, our concept of change is, usually, "exchange." We are like the marine sergeant who clamored: "Men! I have good news and bad news for you! Today we will be changing socks! Johnson, you change with Smith! Smith, you change with Johnson!" We trade bad habits for good ones, at the same time that we trade good habits for bad ones. Our change is not universal and across-the-board. It is "pick and choose" and "mix and match," but not anything that is consistent and absolute. And although all attempts at change are to be encouraged, for indeed we live too imperfect an existence to do an about-face as could once be done, nonetheless, there needs to be a fundamental base to our plan that encompasses all aspects of our existence.

That plan is dependent upon one simple foundation: that we humble ourselves to a Higher Authority and that He become the center of every nuance of our lives in the most personal and intimate way. With this colossal change in attitude as our foundation, those little changes become all the more critical. It is those precious lucid moments, those pristine and pure minutes of clarity, that are at the core of our rehabilitation. It is precisely those momentous decisions when we withstand a challenge, choosing good over evil, that we give G-d great satisfaction and ingratiate us to Him. Whether they are major battles or minor victories over the insurgent foe, they engender the rejuvenation of our closeness to Him that concretizes our determination and solidifies our resolve.

The Talmud says that a person can acquire his eternity in one hour. Some comment that the Hebrew word for "hour" can also mean "turn." Sometimes a small turn in the right direction can inspire a major change. May our hearts always be open to making positive adjustments that are global and universal, albeit small and deliberate. May we endeavor to make G-d the focal point of every aspect of our daily routine, as we systematically make the necessary "turns" toward eternity.

Penitence: How Will I Ever Get There?

A SMALL STEP FOR MAN, A HUGE STEP FOR MANKIND – SO LET'S GET STARTED!

Sam was over an hour late for work again, and his boss called him to task. "Sam! What happened to you today? It's past 10:00 a.m. You're late!"

"Sir, it's not my fault! The weather outside is wild! Rain, sleet, snow, slush, you name it! Why, for every step I took forward, I slipped two steps backward!"

"Sam," his irate boss responded, losing his patience, "if every time you took one step forward you went two steps backward, how in the world did you ever get here?"

"It was simple," Sam responded. "Eventually, I just turned around to go home!"

૭૩૦૨૪૦૪૦

The most difficult aspect of many a task is not the undertaking itself, but beginning it, period. It's hard to get started. Whether it is our natural laziness or a fear of failure, somehow we manage to procrastinate and delay getting even the simplest chores underway. When something is unpleasant and distasteful, it becomes even harder, and there is nothing more difficult than facing one's indiscretions and inconsistencies. Having strayed so far away from the home base – having succumbed to temptation and become its slave – it seems inconceivable to ever return to the innocence of yesteryear, to the simplicity and purity of years past.

In reality, there should be no way to go back in time to make amends for the injudiciousness of the past. What was done was done, never to be retrieved, never to be rectified. The concept of penitence is a novel idea that transcends normative thinking about the present and future versus the past. It is built upon the belief that a person really desires to do that which is right but all too often loses the battle to his evil inclination. When he is inspired to return to the path of righteousness, this spiritual metamorphosis signals his ongoing desire to do what was right all along, and repeals and uproots the misbehavior retroactively.

Indeed it is difficult to change behavior and habits. It is an uphill battle to reverse years of rebelliousness, but it is not an impossible one. Deep down inside a person lies a pure and pristine yearning to act righteously, and all he needs to do is to turn around to go home.

Repentance: Help Me Stop Stealing!

People from New York get a bum rap. I don't know why they have a reputation for being selfish and self-centered. Why, just the other day, I observed two New Yorkers sharing a cab. One guy was taking the battery, and the other guy was taking the tires!

৫৩০৪৪৫০৪৪

Although we might be guilty of many minor indiscretions, most of us are not hard-nosed criminals. We may have our problems with the challenges of envy and the pursuit of honor, not to mention tempering our libido and lustful inclinations, and we most certainly are far from perfect, but generally speaking, we are not robbers and thieves.

Truth be told, however, lying at the core of all our problems is precisely this frailty. We are, in fact, "major" thieves and have been stealing our entire lives! Perhaps the label "thieves" is too harsh, but we certainly are "cheats." Created in the very image of G-d Himself and thereby given a holy soul filled with such great potential, we cheat G-d and we cheat ourselves when, instead of actualizing that spiritual potential, we ignore our innate talents and allow them to atrophy and wither away to skeletal proportions, choosing the easy life instead. Here G-d gave every person the wherewithal to strive for greatness in his own unique way, and instead of nurturing that unlimited force, we starve it to death. We're given diamonds to be polished and cherished, and we treat them like dirt-cheap rock candy.

This is the very question that we need to ask ourselves whenever we contemplate change: What happened to us? Have we lost our perspective? Have we forgotten who we are? Have we lost sight of the secret of our greatness: that we were created in the image of G-d? Have we, too, succumbed to the brainless, heartless hopelessness of a bankrupt society devoid of all spirituality? Have we become petty thieves, common crooks, having stolen a soul with the capacity for greatness and denied it its inherent potential?

Repentance boils down to one thing. We have to stop stealing! We have to stop cheating! We have to stop deceiving ourselves! We have to stop living in a finite, "soulless" dream world, and accept the reality that we are created in G-d's image. We must recognize that we have been gifted with magnificent inner strength that gives us limitless prospects. We must always keep uppermost in our minds the holy words of a great Chassidic Rabbi that the way in which one goes beyond the letter of the law in his observance of the prohibition of "Do not cheat your fellow man" is to avoid cheating oneself!

Freedom of Religion

The Israeli couple has been in line at the bank for over two hours. Oded has no more patience for all of the bureaucracy and announces to his wife, "I can't take this any longer! I've had enough of this! I'm going to the Knesset [Israeli parliament] to kill the prime minister!"

With that, he storms out of the building.

An hour later he returns to the bank. His wife is still in line.

"Where did you go? You ran out of here like a crazy man," she scolds.

"I really went to the Knesset to kill the prime minister. I couldn't take it anymore!"

"So," says his wife, "why didn't you kill him?"

"Are you kidding?" Oded responds. "You should see the line over there!"

છ૭૨૬૭૨૦

We tend to think the grass is greener on the other side of the fence. We make the tragic error of defining our terms by the world's definitions, thinking they have privileged information. Be it Hollywood, the media, or our next-door neighbor, for some strange reason we imagine they have a monopoly on definitions of some of life's most critical concepts. Our pursuit of freedom and opportunity has succumbed to this pattern as well. How many times have we opted to explore their ways, to taste their freedom, rather than to direct our attention to the clear-cut definitions of freedom given to us by the seasoned and sagacious, people who are much wiser and much more well-advised?

Many songs have been sung about freedom, here in "the land of the free." From "Born Free" to "Freedom's Just Another Word for Nothing Left to Lose," the beat may be catchy, but the lyrics can be destructive when distorted and twisted. In truth, the definition of true freedom is founded upon the actualization of potential. We are born to toil, to stretch ourselves and expand, in order to make the greatest contribution possible to the world around us. By tapping into our G-d-given talents and uniqueness and actualizing that endowment to its fullest, we are liberated.

Freedom means to be in control of our destiny, instead of being controlled by forces beyond ourselves. Freedom is achieved when we are able to come in contact with those inimitable forces within, and do not get caught up in the upheaval of an environment that threatens to limit us. We recognize unequivocally that true freedom is much more than just a word, but another world and dimension, through which there is "everything to gain" – both in this world and the next.

How well they have taught us that freedom means to do what you want, when you want, with whom you want, wherever you want, in front of the entire world if you want, and then you will never "want," for it will all be yours. Nothing could be further from the truth.

Growing up in the Western world, we develop many loves and interests. They rapidly become part of us, making detachment quite difficult, if not downright impossible. We are quickly enslaved. With all of our "choices" and "freedoms," we swiftly become entrapped and ensnared to the point of addiction. Without a structure or a discipline, and more importantly, without the inspiration to free our souls from the shackles of their earthly incarceration, we are doomed to live our lives as others would dictate: to dress like them, to speak like them, to be "free" like them.

Do you know when we really will be free? When we toil to refine our character traits, then we will be free. When we are able to control our mouths from utterances of slander and tale bearing, then we will be free. When we can contain our anger and direct the thoughts of our hearts, then we will be free. When we can over-power our inclinations; when we can give up the many loves of our hearts for objectives of much greater importance, then we will be free. When we can finally prioritize our lives, and decide once and for all what is important and what is not, what is eternal and what is a poor substitute, what is essential and what is excess, what will nurture our soul and allow us to actualize its great spiritual potential, and what will lead us in the opposite direction, then we will be free.

When the foundation of our lives will be that which gives the greatest satisfaction to our Creator, then we will be free. Then we will escape the inescapable constraints of a "free world" devoid of true freedom and merit the epitome of freedom: the freedom to have elevated our body to serve its spiritual counterpart, as together they unite in their pursuit of independence.

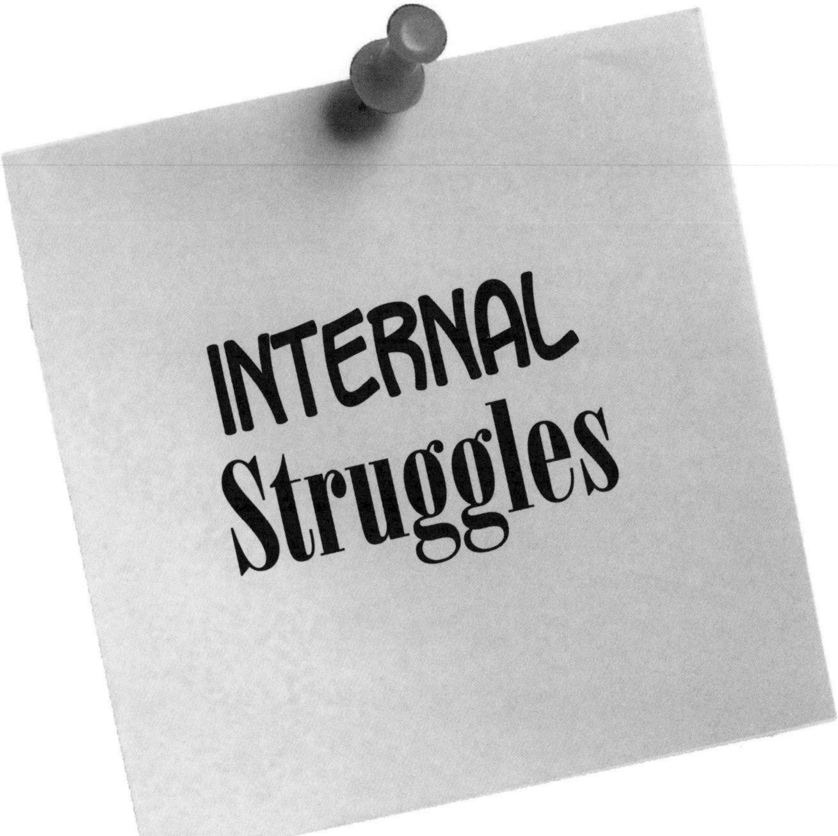
INTERNAL
Struggles

Light and Darkness All in One

THE AGGREGATE OF LIGHT AND DARKNESS IN THE HUMAN PSYCHE GENERATES CONFLICT.

The two women stood before the judge, each one confident that her claim was valid.

It seemed that the same young man had been suggested as a match for both of their daughters. Each mother now claimed that he had been offered to her daughter first, and therefore her daughter reserved the right to marry this boy.

After the women presented their claims, the judge came to a decision. "Being that neither of you can prove which of you was initially contacted regarding this match, I have no recourse but to slice him in half, so that you can share him. Bring the sword!"

"No! No!" screamed out one of the mothers. "I can't allow a human being to die on my account!"

"Kill him!" said the second mother. "It's the only fair thing to do!"

"Ah!" said the judge, addressing the second mother. "The match is yours! You must be the real mother-in-law!"

⋇⋇⋇

Could a person simultaneously broker a marriage and condone the cold-blooded murder of the groom? Absolutely! There are well-dressed, "sophisticated" people who could murder in a suit and tie, careful not to become soiled with their victim's blood, because they are on their way to their kid's PTA meeting. There are senators

91

and congressmen, politicians of all stripes, servants of the people, graduates of the most prestigious universities, who will espouse any policy that will help further their career, regardless how that course of action will endanger their fellow countrymen. There are journalists and members of the media who, contrary to the very creed of their profession, will report the news with absolute bias, to the detriment and jeopardy of their own armed forces and defenders of their very nation. There are members of the clergy who have dedicated their lives to teaching their constituency morality and ethics, who are guilty of the worse indiscretions and licentiousness. How can intelligent people conduct their lives in such total contradiction?

Everyone is familiar with the story of the two women who came before King Solomon with the baby that each claimed to be hers. When the wise King Solomon decreed, by way of compromise, to cut the baby in half, one woman acquiesced and the other begged him not to harm the baby, saying that she would give up her claim to the child if only the king would let the baby live. Consider the psyche of the woman who stole the other's child and was willing to have the child put to death rather than to surrender it to its real mother. At first glance she seems to be the lowest of the low, cold-hearted and frigid. On the other hand, note the pining and yearning this woman must have possessed, to give from her natural wellspring of motherly love and self-sacrifice for the sake of a child, to the point that she was willing to stoop so low in order to fulfill her calling. What kind of pathetic monster is this? A Doctor Jekyll and Mr. Hyde mentality! Can there be anything more brutally cruel than to steal another's infant, and yet anything more admirable than the self-sacrifice of a mother for her child? Can such diametrically opposed behavior coexist in one organism?

We all know people who can simultaneously utter two conflicting statements out of the same side of their mouths. We probably never considered ourselves to be such people, but no doubt, in our thought process, we are all guilty of such dichotomy. After all, we are only human, and this is part of our essence. The battle of light versus darkness in the heart and mind of mankind has been a historical struggle from time immemorial. We must understand that darkness is not simply the absence of light, but a creation in and of itself. Because of this, one could theoretically act like an angel, in a most enlightened fashion, and yet at times exhibit the most degenerative behavior, entrenched in the darkness of this world.

Light and darkness are mutually exclusive and do not operate in the realm of one being contingent on the other. One must struggle to build fortresses of light, and at the same time uproot and remove the darkness. It is not an automatic process. It is therefore possible, and more likely probable, that one could be filled with light yet simultaneously sullied by darkness.

The beginning of solving any problem is contingent on a keen awareness and identification of the problem. Having identified the reality of the coexistence of light and darkness in the human psyche, we need to attack on two fronts with the hope that a little bit of light diffuses a lot of darkness. And each time we rise to the challenge and choose good over bad, each time we overcome and overpower the potential darkness within, we reveal a beacon of light that will illuminate the path to eternity.

Enemies in the West

The knight was reporting on the war effort to the king.

"Your Majesty, we have vanquished your adversaries to the south; we have removed the menace from the east; we have annihilated the opposition in the north; and we have demolished your enemies in the west."

"Enemies in the west?" asked the king. "I don't have any enemies in the west!"

"Well!" replied the knight. "You do now!"

ය ෙ ෙ ෙ

We are forever grateful for the freedom we enjoy in the West that allows us to live our lives and observe our religious practices without concern of persecution. To be sure, though, we would be naive to think that we are free of enemies. Anti-Semitism is on the rise in Western culture. Although not politically correct, bigotry and racism still pervade our culture. Unfair bias and outright slander have infiltrated the shores of democratic societies in the guise of liberalism and taking up the cause of the underdog.

When traced to the core, anti-Semitism and other forms of racism are rooted in nothing more than malevolent hatred and vicious lies. Although it hardly compares to Nazi propaganda – which we thought was excoriated and decried forever but is today taught with venom to impressionable school children throughout the Middle East – the subtle, modern form of racism is similarly rooted and potentially destructive. Nonetheless, we are thankful that the creed of our Western democratic countries is to protect the human rights of all of their citizens without discrimination and prejudice. We only pray that those who champion those rights will be empowered to guarantee the perpetuation of democracies in the spirit of fairness, equality, and tolerance as intended at their founding.

However, we face another enemy in the West. Ironically, that enemy is the very freedom we enjoy, and it has contributed to a spiritual genocide of catastrophic proportions across the religious spectrum. Of course, it goes without saying that we wouldn't trade our freedom for anything in the world; we dare not suggest that we would be better off as the constituents of some dogmatic communist regime or that we would prefer to live under the threat of dictatorship and autocratic rule. Nonetheless, we would be foolish to ignore the battle that our freedom creates, which threatens our very eternity.

Today, we are bombarded with shells of visual ammunition that pull us into a world where the evil inclination has free reign. And even when that attack is not fully invasive in the physical realm, nonetheless, our minds and our hearts are inundated by this formidable foe, and we find ourselves living a vicarious existence steeped in promiscuity. There isn't a child who is not exposed to all of the decadence and debauchery the world has to offer. Thanks to the Internet and massive international communications – and our own folly in allowing our homes to become entertainment centers offering licentiousness of every sort – the chances of bringing up a child who is wholesome and somewhat protected are miniscule, if not zero. What are we to do?

One thing is for sure. Abandonment is not the answer. Freedom is one thing; total nihilism is quite another. There must be a structure to our lives, a hierarchy to our priorities, a cap on our vulnerability, a discipline to our inalienable rights. There are things that need not be seen, experiences that we can do without. Nobody is better off having experienced virtual violence through the latest video-game monster, certainly not a child.

When I was a kid, my parents didn't even allow toy guns in the house. Need I mention what we expose our children to through movies and videos where the wholesomeness of love and courtship of yesteryear has been replaced with libidos gone wild, giving license to every conceivable type of immoral arrangement that legitimizes the illegitimate and creates a distorted sense of priorities? As my teacher used to say, "We have become so open-minded that our brains have fallen out." What are we thinking when we allow our children full access to Internet communication without restraint in the privacy of their rooms?

But the real question is not "What are we doing to our children?" Rather, it is "What are we doing to ourselves?" If we don't take the necessary steps to control our own lives, we will never be able to influence our children. Wholesomeness is not "nerdy." It is the greatest gift we can pass down to them. Indeed, when we take our freedom and structure it in a way that allows for our optimal spiritual growth, we will have combined two great gifts to create a human being whose productivity is eternal, and the freedom of the West will be our greatest friend.

Just One Word

True story:

A young journalist was sitting next to the laconic US president Calvin Coolidge (famously known as Silent Cal) at a banquet, and he turned to him mischievously.

"Mr. President, I have a bet with my editor that I can get you to say more than two words this evening."

Mr. Coolidge responded, "You lose!"

ෆහ෫ඏ෨

Wisdom's best protector is silence. Much can be lost with more than two words, or even one. Worlds and people can be destroyed; lives can be uprooted. It is not necessarily verbosity and loquaciousness that cause upheaval; sometimes it is a mere extraneous word or two that results in damage and detriment. Our insensitivity, or our tendency to be judgmental, can easily disrupt a courtship, ruin one's livelihood, or destroy a friendship.

It's not only what we say that counts, but also what we don't say. All too often, inferences are deduced, tones of voice are interpreted, facial expressions are read, and before we know it we have discouraged and disparaged without even trying to do so. We've evolved into a garrulous society that speaks indiscriminately, irresponsibly, and, increasingly, abusively. Name-calling, bad-mouthing, and foul language is run-of-the-mill and thereby an inevitable part of our children's vernacular. Choice of words is no longer of significance.

Indeed, the importance of the spoken word has been cheapened. The repercussions of this can be tragic and long-lasting.

But as much as a negative word can be destructive, a positive word can give life. A warm greeting to a newcomer, an encouraging word, a simple compliment – all of these can inject an infusion of life into the bloodstream of their recipient in an act that is G-dly in nature, for it mimics He Who is acclaimed as the One Who gives life to all that exists.

For those meticulous about their speech, each word becomes a challenge: what to say and what to avoid saying, when to say something and when to refrain from speaking or postpone it for a more propitious moment. In effect, each spoken (or unspoken) word becomes a spiritual contest, affording us many opportunities to rise to the occasion and reap great eternal reward throughout the day.

Man's Worst Friend

WE MUST BE A GOOD FRIEND TO OURSELVES.

In a last-minute huddle, the three men sentenced to be executed by the firing squad decided on a plan for their salvation. A moment before the end, they would scream out the name of some natural disaster, with the hope that everyone would drop his weapons, and run for his life.

The English gentleman was to be first. As they counted down: "10, 9, 8, 7, 6... ready..., " he yelled, "earthquake! Run for your lives!" In a matter of seconds the crowd dispersed, and the condemned man ran to safety.

The firing squad reassembled, and the Australian was brought next. As the firing squad readied for execution, the accused screamed out, "Tornado! Run for your lives," and again everyone fled, including the condemned man, who ran to safety.

The firing squad reassembled again, and the American from Brooklyn was brought in for execution. As they counted down: "10, 9, 8, 7, 6, 5, 4, 3, 2, 1, ready! aim!" he screamed out, "fire!"

એ૧૨૨૪જી

At times we are our worst enemies and bring about our own downfall. You'd think we would know better than to engage in self-destructive deprecation, but notwithstanding how nonsensical it may be, we beat up on ourselves in a way that is counterproductive and debilitating. One could well imagine the upheaval to the career of the professional baseball player who cannot get past the error he made that let in the winning run, or the limited future of the quarterback who continues to lament the interception he threw that cost his team the game. Any manager or coach who is worth his weight would tell his player to put it behind him and get on with life. "Everyone makes mistakes. Don't let it destroy your future and undermine your great potential."

The person who was dismissed from his employment must go on to the next interview and not drown in his personal sorrow; the spouse whose marriage went sour and ended in divorce must get past his intense disappointment and build toward the future. Even tragedy cannot interfere in the productivity of a human being, and somehow must be transformed into a building block for the future. We cannot afford to, nor may we, allow dissatisfaction, mistakes, or even failure to destroy our confidence and belief in our G-d-given talents and natural abilities.

If this is true in the physical realm of existence, it certainly pertains to the spiritual realm. Every year we are faced with the many failures of the past year and years gone by. The reality of our injudiciousness and outright rebellion is more than we can bear. Our many broken promises and sanctimoniousness is a hypocrisy that stabs us in the gut and shatters what's left of our spiritual self-esteem. The evil inclination, never one "to waste a good crisis opportunity" (Rahm Emanuel, 2009), jumps on the occasion before him, to crush us and bring us to despair. We find ourselves dispirited, and unable to go on. How dare we come before our Creator again with promises to repent when our track record is so bad? What is the limit? How much can He endure? Is there no throttle to our audaciousness? Is there no boundary to our unmitigated impudence?

It is precisely at this point that we must recognize that regardless of the indiscretions of the past and the numerous times we felt forced to cave in to the enemy who was unrelenting and indefatigable, we have never faced the true essence of that formidable foe until now. It is this force of impending hopelessness that is his forte. He may be a general practitioner with multiple talents and disguises, but imposing hopelessness is his specialty. He now has us where he wants us, and will soon destroy any remnant of hope for the future. He has achieved the ultimate. He has won us over to his side. We are now aiding and abetting the enemy. He can afford to let us go and attend to his business, for he knows that once we have fallen into the ugly claws of resignation and surrender we will finish off the job for him and destroy ourselves. We are in great danger! Despondency sets in, and utter despair is just around the corner. What are we to do?

The answer lies in replicating the ways of G-d Himself. The Talmud instructs: "Just as He is merciful, so shall you be merciful; just as He is compassionate, so shall you be compassionate." And perhaps we can add: Just as He "raises the needy from the dust, and from the trash heaps He lifts up the destitute to seat them among the nobles, the nobility of His people," so shall we. Just as He elevates the poorest and most removed, so must we.

All charity begins at home, so we must begin with ourselves. We must catapult our low spirit to safer grounds that defy despair and resist such pessimism. And much like our Creator does, we must lift our own spirits high, and set our sights on nobility and aristocracy of the highest accord. We must remove ourselves from the clutches of hopelessness and utter devastation, with a renewed belief in our self-worth and a new lease on life. We must be a good friend to our own selves, and inspire within us a determination to climb that ladder of spiritual success, with our faith in mankind restored and our spiritual confidence regenerated.

Not So Fast

The drill sergeant was dismissing his men when he casually mentioned to Goldberg, "By the way, Goldberg, your best friend just got killed in action."

The lieutenant, having observed the sergeant's insensitivity, called him to task and blasted him for his callousness.

The next day, the sergeant received word that Goldberg's grandmother had passed away. Before he dismissed his men, he yelled out, "Hey, Goldberg, your grandma kicked the bucket this morning!"

Again, the sergeant was sharply rebuked by his commanding officer for his insensitivity.

A week later, the sergeant was about to dismiss his men when he was handed a telegram in regard to the sudden passing of Goldberg's father. Concerned that he not be reprimanded by the lieutenant again, he resolved to treat the matter with greater sensitivity. He announced, "Men! Now listen here! All those who have both parents living take one step forward! Not so fast, Goldberg!"

વ્ઝ૩ૹૹ

We have been taught that one should not be the bearer of bad news. This directive not only stresses the importance of sensitivity regarding such delicate matters, but also offers us practical advice how to convey such news, so that its recipient can adapt in a gradual fashion. By being somewhat indirect and vague, the sad news is absorbed in increments, which allows for the necessary adjustment. Such is the nature of man.

Man has the uncanny ability to adapt and acclimate himself to the most dire situations. People who survived various disasters and upheavals will tell you that their survival rested on their ability to adapt. Those who prevailed through the horrors of Nazi concentration camps certainly invoked this means as a key to their forbearance and ultimate survival. Without the ability to adapt we would find it impossible to endure our ever-changing lives.

However this very character trait that allows for man's survival is, at times, his undoing. Precious moments of inspiration are lost, indelible impressions fade away, because man adapts so well – too well! And although that too is human nature, man must work steadfastly to ensure that he remains an inspired individual and not succumb to the malaise of "old hat" and complacency. Otherwise, familiarity will breed contentment, which in turn suffocates any spark of inspiration. How, then, does one remain inspired, when routine wears away at those sparks that have been stirred and renders them unremarkable and routine?

There was a man by the name of Palti ben Layish who merited special Heavenly intervention that allowed him to escape a dreadful sin. The daughter of King Saul was wed to David through a marriage ceremony that David considered legally correct, but Saul held to be invalid. Deeming her to be unmarried, Saul proceeded to marry her off to Palti, who understood that his "new wife" was quite possibly someone else's wife.

Palti, who feared Heaven, made a determination there and then that he would not touch this woman (his "new wife"). In order to concretize his commitment, he thrust a sword in the bed between the two of them and asserted, "Whoever [referring to himself] involves himself with this woman shall be pierced by this sword." It was due to this noble act that he merited Heavenly intervention and was able to escape a grave transgression.

What exactly was so great about thrusting a sword into the bed between them? Was that really going to prevent him from becoming intimate with this woman in the almost inevitable eventuality of his desire for her overwhelming him, during the many years they were together? All he needed to do was to remove the sword, go around the sword, or just simply ignore it. What practical purpose did it serve, and why did this act warrant such support from Heaven?

It has been explained as follows: Palti knew that his momentary determination and steadfast commitment would not last forever. He knew that many a weak moment would befall him on the road ahead. He needed to do something to physically express his sincere conviction at that moment, to act as a perpetual reminder, that there was a time when he had felt so strongly about this matter – that there had been a time when he possessed the strength to overcome all obstacles.

In the spirit of the dictum that one needs to take inspiration and immediately transfer and express it in a physical object, Palti thrust all of his determination into that sword and declared: "If I should ever dare to touch my new wife, I shall be worthy of death. And at moments of weakness, I will look at that sword, the symbol of my strength, and revert back to that lucid and spirited auspicious moment. I will be reminded of what I once possessed, and will become reinvigorated to withstand the temptation. And in doing so, I will have defeated the malaise of adaptation, my flame reignited, my confidence restored."

Palti's genius was the revelation that we don't have to succumb to the malaise of routine, that those priceless moments of inspiration need not be lost. We can reconnect to them and regain that spiritual energy. When those treasured moments come our way, we pray that they not dissipate, but instead linger. Let them jar our memory to be recalled and reignited, and leave us indelibly inspired as once before. Inspiration might be fleeting and dissolve too fast, but it's never too late to retrieve it.

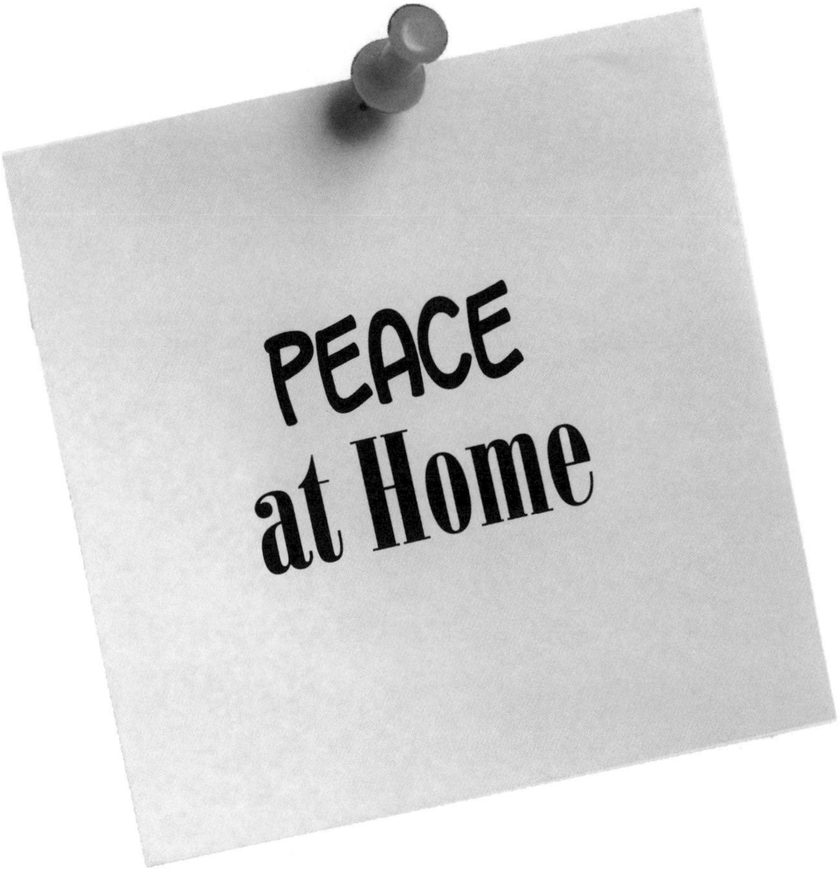
PEACE
at Home

Amalgamation and Integration

A man approaches the only other patron in a bar and asks if he could buy him a drink.

"Why, of course!" comes the reply.

The first man then asks, "Where are you from?"

"I'm from Nebraska," replies the second man.

The first man responds, "I can't believe it! I'm from Nebraska too! Let's have another round to Nebraska."

Curious, the first man asks, "Which city?"

"Omaha," the second man answers.

"I can't believe it. I'm from Omaha too," the first man responds. "Bartender, send a round of drinks in honor of Omaha."

The second man then asks the first, "What school did you attend?"

"Omaha Tech P.S. 123," the first man answers. "What about you?"

"By golly, Omaha Tech P.S. 123," the second man replies.

"This is unbelievable," says the first man. "Let me ask you one more question: What year did you graduate?"

"Class of '62," the second man answers.

"Me too!" says the first man incredulously.

Meanwhile a third patron walks into the bar, sits down on a stool, and says to the bartender: "What's going on today?

Anything new?"

"Same old thing," answers the bartender. "It has been a pretty slow crowd. Oh yeah," pointing to the other two patrons, "the Johnson twins are drunk again!"

ଓଓଡ୍ଡ

Two great Talmudic scholars debate the allowance for any leeway in the praising of the bride to the groom at their wedding. One opinion insists that one must not exaggerate her merits, but rather "tell it as it is." According to this opinion: "The praise of the bride should be according to who she is." He must find some virtue that is absolutely true, and articulate it without embellishment. The other opinion remains adamant that the bride be complimented to the hilt, as one who is both beautiful and pious, no matter her true state of resplendency. "But, how could one lie?" the first opinion asks the second. "Isn't the commandment abundantly clear in its instruction that one distance oneself from all that is false?" The second opinion responds with the proverbial dictum: "A person's mindset must always be interwoven with that of others," and he must thereby be sensitive to their predicament. One who is mindful of the groom's obvious enchantment with the bride can honestly say that she possesses a special charm and beauty regardless of his own impression, for he empathizes with the heart of his brother. This is no lie. This is the greatest truth.

Not only is this not a falsehood, it is the requisite manner in which people should act. When a person has already made a decision, acquired a purchase, cut the deal, we should commend his judgment, congratulate him on his acquisition, and wish him well. In short, give him strength! Give him life!

The thought occurred to me that there is a reason this lesson is being taught to us specifically when discussing the proper conduct for rejoicing before a bride and groom. It is to teach a monumental principle for marital bliss. At the very inception of this new merger, we want to reinforce the importance of interconnecting, of thinking of the other, and commiserating with his mentality. If any two people should be mindful of the importance of being sensitive to, and cognizant of, one another's feelings and thinking processes, it is a husband and wife. It is this new unit of one diverse being that needs to personify this trait to perfection. When a couple's relationship is built upon a strong emphasis on endeavoring to always understand from where each one is coming and the background upon which his or her particular view is based, they will find a natural homogenization to their bond, and an inevitable fusion will form in their newly found harmonious world.

Imagine a situation in which a wife goes to great lengths to prepare dinner for her husband, and instead of complimenting her for her efforts and the delectable food, he begins by showering his plate with salt and pepper, and proceeds to complain that the food is not sufficiently warm. Or consider the following scenario: A husband has the rare opportunity to speak at a family gathering. On the way home that night he asks his wife for some feedback on his speech. The wife begins to take apart the speech from beginning to end. "The first joke bombed, the second one didn't connect, the message was over everyone's head, and you forgot to mention the hosts."

In each of these cases, one spouse was looking for support from the other, and instead received ridicule and derision. The failure of this husband to go beyond himself and to perceive how hard his wife worked to make him a scrumptious supper, and the great amount of pride and love that went into its preparation, is unacceptable. He is clearly caught up in himself and is guilty of not being empathetic with what went through her mind. The wife who took apart her husband's speech didn't put herself in his place to understand his nervousness prior to his speech, and the satisfaction he felt in having delivered it. This too resulted from a lack of being properly interconnected. In the place of the support he needed ("Great speech! Everyone was listening!"), he got a slap in the face.

To be properly interconnected, one needs to be fine-tuned and possess an exceptionally sensitive ear. He or she needs to be not only one who foresees the future, but one who is keenly aware of what has already transpired.

I am reminded of a remarkable story about a Chassidic Rebbe walking with his attendant in the streets of Tel Aviv. Walking down a street filled with many stores, they had just past a jewelry store when the Rebbe tells his attendant that he wants to go into the store to purchase a gift for his wife. The attendant is puzzled by the Rebbe's uncharacteristic request to shop in a Tel Aviv jewelry store, but nonetheless accompanies the Rebbe into the store. What happens next is even more perplexing. The Rebbe asks the man behind the counter to show him very expensive necklaces, and as he is shown tray after tray, he consistently expresses his total dissatisfaction with all that is displayed. "Isn't there anyone here who has some discernment in jewelry, who can show me something in good taste?" the Rebbe exclaims, with what appears to be contempt for the proprietor's lack of good judgment.

"My wife is in the back," the proprietor responds, and he calls her out to show the Rebbe some jewelry. Whatever the man's wife brings out to show the Rebbe meets with the Rebbe's approval, and he compliments her with great acclaim. "Now here is a person who has good taste in jewelry," the Rebbe declares with a smile, and proceeds to purchase an expensive diamond necklace, way beyond his means.

Months later, the attendant musters up the courage to ask the Rebbe to explain his bizarre behavior. The Rebbe responds: "As we were passing by that store, didn't you hear the man berating his wife, chiding her for buying jewelry that will not sell, and that because of her poor judgment they are stuck with merchandise that they can't move! The anger and abusive language was appalling! I could not allow this man's wife to suffer such scorn."

The Rebbe's unusually refined and sensitive ears picked this up on a noisy street in Tel Aviv, and he immediately put his plan into action to bolster the esteem of a wife in the eyes of her husband.

This Rebbe's heart, like so many other great people like him, incorporated the hearts of those around him. It was inextricably linked to the suffering of others and was profoundly connected to them.

His was an act of one who was attuned to the thought process and plight of the other, of one who had achieved a level of excellence that was impeccable and flawless, a masterful display of refinement. In the story above, the piece of jewelry purchased shone with great brilliance, but it was superseded by the brilliant shine of the Rebbe, so fine and so sensitive, so interconnected.

Communication

Mr. Kartoffel went to the same restaurant in the Lower East Side every day for nearly thirty years. He always ordered the same thing: a bowl of chicken soup, a sweet roll, and a black coffee.

One day, after the waiter had served him the usual, Mr. Kartoffel called him over and said, "Vaiter, I vant you should taste mein soup!"

The waiter was quite taken aback and said, "Why do you want me to taste your soup?"

"I vant you should taste mein soup," Mr. Kartoffel insisted even more emphatically.

"What's wrong with the soup?" the waiter inquired, which only prompted Mr. Kartoffel to demand again, in an even stronger tone, "I vant you should taste mein soup!"

"Mr. Kartoffel, you've ordered the same soup for thirty years. What could be wrong with it now?" the waiter responded, somewhat agitated.

Again Mr. Kartoffel demanded, "I vant you should taste mein soup!"

Exasperated, the waiter sighed and reached for the spoon, but couldn't find it. "Hey! Mr. Kartoffel," he asked, "where is your spoon?"

With a grin on his face, Mr. Kartoffel responded, "Ahaaa!"

In spite of the importance of the art of proper communication in the building of relationships, there are many people who never seem to master that art, and because of lack of communication, their relationships suffer. Some are poor communicators because their parents didn't communicate well. Others may fail in this interactional area of relationships due to some personality flaw that bars the openness essential for a complementary exchange and indispensable for a reciprocal give-and-take.

Whatever the cause, there is no question that communication is a tool of critical urgency that must be mastered if one is to maximize the success of the many critical relationships during the course of one's life. Parents and children, husbands and wives, in-laws, sons-in-law and daughters-in-law, teachers and students, bosses and employees, and good friends all need to exchange ideas and articulate their thoughts in a clear, polite, and expressive manner. Otherwise, chaos reigns, as miscommunications wreak havoc on these vital alliances of love, mutual respect, and affection.

Not hating your brother in your heart demands that you should either be big enough to forgive and forget, or else be able to talk things out with your friend and reconcile differences. Never is there an allowance for hatred, except perhaps toward a notorious and unusually evil person. Unwarranted hatred is called "hatred for no reason," for in fact there is no reason for it. Either speak it out or let it go, but don't harbor it in your heart. Communicate your feelings, albeit with softness and respect, yet without inhibition. Don't be afraid to express yourself, and don't be afraid to listen to, and seriously consider, the other party's view.

One could readily imagine how detrimental the lack of communication can be in a marriage. The uniting of two people as one in marriage has been described as two people working together to reach wholeness. Through the bond of marriage and the inevitable communication that is essential to its success, each partner learns about his own strengths and weaknesses, as he interacts with his spouse in an ongoing learning and growing experience that helps to actualize his potential to its fullest. Good communication lies at the core of this growth process, as the couple hone their skills in the articulation of ideas and the art of listening attentively. As their relationship matures, they learn to trust that they will be understood with the greatest of sensitivity and care. Even at moments of dissonance and variance that are to be expected, their bond of communication will enable them to not only work out their differences, but actually to proliferate and become all the bigger.

Communication demands a keen understanding of the other side. It's not merely the expression of ideas, but the exchange of ideas, with attentive listening as much an integral element as coherent articulation. On the many occasions that I have acted as a third party in speaking to couples (dating and beyond), I found that my job, as I saw it, was to ensure that there be communication between the two parties; that they indeed respond to each other's comments and questions, and not go off on a tangent; that they listen to what the other one was saying, and not interrupt in the middle; that they talk to the point and address the matter before them, instead of going off the handle onto something peripheral. I found myself constantly asking them to repeat what the other had said, to make sure that they were in fact listening. Two things became clear: they had not been communicating, and that with a little adjustment (in these cases, the presence of a third party, who made sure of it), they actually understood one another, giving hope that their differences could be worked out.

I've met with couples during the dating process with the hope that through the auspices of an objective third party to echo and rephrase their attempts at communication, it would bring clarity to their doubts. These meetings are long (usually three hours – it takes time to communicate) and intense (I try to make it pleasant), and thankfully, have been productive. I write all this not in order to hand out a business card, but to make one point: communication really does work!

The punishment of the "generation of the tower," who dared to wage war against G-d in a display of audacious defiance of the omnipotence of the Master of the Universe, was a communication breakdown. A request for a hammer was answered with a trowel, a brick with a box-lunch, a straight screwdriver with a Phillips screwdriver. A basic tenet in the understanding of the ways of G-d is that He punishes one measure for another. This means that the type of punishment meted out to the transgressor is commensurate to the wrongdoing so that the sinner will understand where he went wrong. G-d's intent in punishment is to rehabilitate and not to exact vengeance. How, then, was this punishment meted out against this recalcitrant generation of rebels, one measure for another?

The answer to this question lies at the very core of mankind's purpose on this earth: the recognition of his Creator, and the dissemination and circularization of His glory. When a person sees through the facade of this world and allows his inner self to connect to his Creator, then he has communicated on the highest level. When instead he succumbs to the malaise of the belief that "it is my own strength and the force of my hand that has achieved all of this power and success," so well-personified in today's rebellious generation, then he has experienced the ultimate communication breakdown.

We need to communicate on every level so that we will excel in the relationship of all relationships. Our success with our relationships is a precursor to success in our relationship with G-d. We dare not refrain from the exertion of every ounce of energy to ensure that we communicate with all of our heart and soul, to our Father in Heaven.

Home Sweeт Home

"Don't forget we are moving today. If you come home to this house this afternoon, it will be empty!" Professor Jones's wife told her absent-minded husband.

Predictably, the professor forgot all about it and returned to the vacated house that afternoon, without any recollection whatsoever as to where his family had moved. He went outside, to the front of the house, where he found a little girl playing.

"Excuse me! Did you happen to see a moving van parked in front of this house today?"

"Yes," she replied.

"Do you remember what time it was here?" he asked.

"I think it was around three this afternoon," she replied.

"Do you happen to know which way it went?" he asked.

Looking up at him, she answered, "Yes, Daddy, I'll show you exactly where it went!"

ೞೞೞೞ

People, who are on their best behavior in the company of others – at the workplace, school, or supermarket – will let down all barriers in the comfort of their homes. The idea that someone with a sterling reputation in the eyes of others could act and speak coarsely and almost abusively to his own wife and children is an anomaly that requires explanation. Has he forgotten who they are? Does he not remember that these are his precious loved ones who are his best friends and most devoted advocates? Does he suddenly draw a blank on all of their devotion and dedication, and the joy they have brought him? What prompts him to speak and act so gently and "sweet" outside of his home, while at home he sometimes resembles a raving madman?

The same gentleman who works on himself to strike the proper balance in his conduct with others can be totally off-balance as he lets his hair down in, of all places, his home. Even those who have the sensitivity to turn their homes into a sanctuary of sorts, and preserve its dignity, can somehow forget to include speech and deed in that endeavor. The self-control and discipline that sustains the well-mannered gets lost in the clutter of the homestead.

"It's human nature," we will say. "Everyone's like that!"

We concern ourselves with the impression we make on others and how we will look in their eyes, when in truth our conduct will have its deepest effect on those closest to us. One way or another, that behavior pattern will come back to haunt us. Children learn through osmosis. Our outbursts could one day become theirs. Our choice of words might very well become part of their vernacular. It's frightening to see our children repeat our mistakes, especially when we were their inspiration. In the heat of an argument we might speak to our spouses in tones that would be unthinkable if it were a disagreement with others. And in the end we hurt those who are closest to us in a pervading and penetrating way. It may be human nature, but it is unacceptable for a person of nobility.

There is a gross distortion of reality that carries over to our relationships in the privacy of our homes. In that setting, removed from outside observers (with the exception of our family members) we feel unfettered of the fear of others. We can be ourselves! Would it only be that we would act at home as we act in front of others. If only our interactions with our family members would be treated with the same scrutiny and sensitivity as are those with friends and associates. Surely, we know that there is no privacy that excludes G-d, no domain free of His presence. There is no excuse for absentmindedness, but rather we must know and appreciate where we live, with whom we live, and make our homes a model for all that is good.

Marital Talk

A famous humorist once said about his marriage: "It first occurred to me that our marriage might be in trouble when my wife won an all-expenses-paid vacation for two to Hawaii, and she went twice!"

ॐ

How sad it is when relationships go sour and husbands and wives begin to live separate lives. What promised to be a relationship crowned by a harmonious blend of interdependency and symbiosis of the highest order can become a "relationship" of disassociation, when self-sufficiency and personal autonomy surface their ugly heads and destroy all consonance and congruity. Somewhere along the way, communication breaks down, and fertile soil with so much potential for productivity turns into consolidated bedrock and impenetrable terrain. Where did it all begin?

All too often, it began right at the beginning. In order to recognize the initial stages of communication breakdown, one must understand what good communication is all about. As a novice, each party is likely to have unrealistic expectations and misconceptions about proper communication that could lead to disappointment and disarray. It is not uncommon for one to think he is being communicative when, in fact, he is unexpressive and holding much inside. Some people are naturally more articulate than others. Some are less inclined to open up, while some are products of homes where parents themselves were uncommunicative. The innate differences between the emotional make-ups of a man and a woman inevitably impact this situation. The paramount importance of building trust in the initial months and years of a marriage can be marred by this problem, and can lead to destructive fallout in its wake.

Good communication demands time and patience – and good listening skills. It requires clear expression and thought-out enunciation of ideas. It necessitates a mutual respect that fosters an attentive ear and a relaxation of one's restlessness. "Schmoozing" with one's spouse is as important as discussions of earth-shattering problems. The confidence that is built through the mundane talk of these beloved friends is crucial to the success of every couple's future, and is, in fact, not mundane at all, but holy.

When couples commit to give an attentive ear to one another and articulate their feelings with great sensitivity and concern, they fulfill the dictate of "Love your brother as you love yourself" in the ideal sense. When they are careful to choose their words carefully by using language that is clean and refined – and upbeat – the mutual respect developed through that medium goes a long way toward promoting peace and tranquility. When each spouse recognizes that his or her communication with the other is not simply an act of kindness, but rather a manifestation of the symphonic phenomenon of "one's spouse is like his or her own being" – and that he most assuredly would never fail to give himself the proper attention – the relationship will flourish, and that inseparable bond will be formed.

Marriages require constant reinforcement. There is no limit to the amount of times that one's love and affection for one's partner in life can, and should, be expressed. Nothing is cheapened in the process. The bond is only strengthened. The inability of one mate or both to be positively expressive and complimentary is a communication breakdown that demands rectification.

In a sense the closeness that evolves in this ongoing 24/7 relationship unmasks one spouse to the other in a way that can be compared to an exposed nerve beneath a decayed tooth that requires the attention of a dentist. The sensations felt by virtue of that vulnerability demand a delicate hand, extreme sensitivity, and constant reassurance. When the dentist says: "You're doing great, you're a real soldier," or "We're almost finished," his encouragement helps his patient weather the storm and rejuvenates his resolve to withstand the excruciating pain, until the job is done.

A couple that is expressive and free-flowing about their feelings of love and respect for one another are in turn giving one another the strength to withstand the temporary pain of the eruptions from their occasional, yet inevitable, variance and discord. In those moments of dissension, a wrong word, even unintended, can go straight to the nerve, or even worse, can stab through the heart. The ongoing reinforcement and support allow these painful moments to dissipate, and the bond of the strength of that love and respect to regenerate.

In this sense, talk is not cheap. It makes all the difference in the world in securing the success of the most important interpersonal relationship of one's lifetime.

Sailing the Seven C's of Child Rearing

SEVEN RULES TO FOLLOW IN RAISING CHILDREN.

The Sunday school teacher was projecting her own heretical views, when she asked her class if they really believed that Jonah was swallowed by a whale and survived.

Little Sarah, unabashed, was brave enough to respond, "Yes! I believe every word of it!"

"Well, how will you prove that it is true?" the dissident teacher asked.

Sarah, not hesitating for a moment, answered, "When I get to Heaven, I'm going to ask Jonah myself!"

"But how do you know that Jonah is in Heaven?" asked the teacher. "Maybe he's in the other place?"

Sarah didn't flinch. "Then you ask him!"

ೞೞೞೞ

Children are bright, resourceful, and quite perceptive, very often putting us adults to shame. One thing is for sure: any parent, teacher, or educator who thinks for a moment that he is "merely dealing with a child" underestimates and misunderstands the "absorbent sponge" and pure-minded phenomenon that stands before him. Everything we do and say will be soaked up by this precious child, either through his sharp senses or through the process of osmosis. We adults better be on our best behavior, lest our children's lasting impressions of us come back to haunt us one day.

What follows are the 7 C's of child rearing – seven principles that remind us how to act in order to teach our children.

1) Conduct: Ours! The way we act and conduct our lives will reflect immeasurably on our children and students. A father who spends time with his children, who is warm and loving, who is a bastion of strength for them emotionally and spiritually, who exemplifies integrity and fairness, who sets a tone of calm and equanimity in the home, who is optimistic and encouraging, will reap the rewards of his efforts. A mother who talks softly, even when things are tense, who is careful about her dignity and modesty, who opens her home to guests and involves herself in the needs of the community, who showers her family with motherly tenderness, will find that her mark has been made on her children in the most unobtrusive and natural way. A couple who speak respectfully to one another even when in disagreement, whose shared love and devotion is apparent in word and in deed, whose relationship is built upon mutual respect, evenhandedness, selflessness, and self-sacrifice, will merit to see children who build homes founded on peace and tranquility.

Children who are privileged to grow up in a home where family dinners are not mere extras; where slandering another is never an option; where a disparaging word about someone's speech, or even the neighbor's lawn, is nonexistent; where the talk is positive and upbeat, filled with praise and encouragement and tolerance and acceptance; where there is an outpouring of love and affection; will inhale that atmosphere and absorb it into their bloodstream.

Imagine the impression it makes upon children who see their parents answer all phone calls, never instructing "tell them I'm not home." How fortunate is the child who grows up in an environment of great enthusiasm about doing for others, where charity is given with joy and generosity, where the glory of the G-d and the magnificent world He created is spoken about without inhibition, where the flaunting of an ostentatious and pretentious lifestyle is abhorred, no matter what one's fiscal status. When our conduct will be exemplary, we will merit to see the transmission of all that we hold dear to our greatest treasure – our precious children.

2) Cognizance: An awareness of the greatness of the gift of children is essential in the education process. In a world that has decided that children are a hassle and interfere with their parents' chosen self-serving or career-consuming lifestyle, we must be unequivocal about the priority we place on our progeny and their development. We are here to toil and to build our own small world, and our children and grandchildren are the pillar and backbone of that edifice. Every ounce of energy and resources that we invest into our children will enhance that structure and enable us to build that world.

It is no simple matter that the Sages of the Talmud compare one not blessed with children to one who is dead, for they are our life, our future, and the object of our purpose on this earth. They allow us to fulfill our innate and natural inclination and yearning to give, as we give to that which we helped create, having been granted the privilege to collaborate with the Creator of all that exists, in a partnership for posterity. They allow us the opportunity to imitate and emulate G-d, albeit in a miniscule way, in the manner in which He continuously sustains life. And it goes without saying that they are the source of our greatest pride and joy, which fills our hearts with even more love for them. Each one of them is a precious gift from G-d, for which we are eternally grateful.

3) Cuddling: We must display our love for our children by showering them with tenderness. Our warm embrace, our demonstrative show of affection, insulates, encourages, and secures a bond not easily broken. There is no limit to the amount of love and encouragement we can give our children. This should be our general demeanor, notwithstanding the importance of discipline, which is equally a show of love. Compliments and the accentuation of the positive should be the creed of our interaction with our children. Criticism should be carefully lined in silk, patiently delayed for the propitious moment.

We should remember that our children are always our "babies" who need the cuddling and the comforting contact of those who have nurtured their growth. As I look back to my own parents of blessed memory, I realize that even as a fully grown middle-aged man, I so miss their warm hugs and kisses, the strength they constantly infused in me. Our children must be told how much we love and cherish them, how each one is special and unique. Never should they doubt our belief in them, for they look to us for that strength. We dare not disappoint them.

4) Courtesy: You may be thinking: Show respect to your kids? You must be kidding! Not in the least! It is wrong to embarrass any person, including minors. There surely are occasions that warrant discipline, for the sake of fostering the good of the child. But it is all too common that the damage caused by disciplining exceeds the benefit. One could achieve much more by following the path of showing honor and gentleness. A child is a real person with real feelings that should be handled with the utmost sensitivity. He may readily accept his fate as a member of the "small" community, nevertheless the build-up of incessantly being squashed and disrespected can take its toll and evolve into unresolved frustration, and ultimate resentment.

The teenager whose opinion is just pushed under the rug, or written off as some uncontrollable hormonal whim, without discussion and explanation, will likely be heard saying, "My parents hate me," which may very well mean "My parents don't respect me." There is no question that discipline and direction are crucial to every child's development, but there is a major difference between imposed despotism that dehumanizes, and mutually respectful instruction that builds character. When dealing with my students who are lax about their attendance, I first tell them how much I missed them in their absence. Then I ask them to explain their disappearance. The message is clear: "I'm concerned about your lapses, but I haven't lost my love and respect for you." Children must feel our respect for them, and in doing so, we will imbue in them a monumental lesson in honoring parents.

5) Consolation: Our children need to know that they can turn to us for everything. We need to engage them in conversation, and spend time "schmoozing" with them, in order to establish a rapport and create an open line of communication. The development of trust between parent and child is essential in order that the parent's words will have an impact upon his children. As with any relationship, the degree to which one party will seek the other's council is directly linked to their level of mutual trust and respect. Although our children are not our peers, they should be made to feel the bond of our unlimited friendship and our listening ear. They should find in their parents the comfort they seek to allay their fears, and the solace needed to ease their tension. In the healthiest of parent-child relationships, the parent never ceases to be a parent and remains that special source of consolation and strength to his children of any age.

6) Crisis Management: At times we need to ride the storm and do our best at maintaining stability and equilibrium. No matter how many books one reads on child rearing, nobody is the perfect parent, and mistakes are inevitable. Certainly, the teenage years present the greatest challenge, with damage control often becoming the focus, more so than instruction and direction. At times of crisis, it is crucial that we keep the lines of communication open and display our genuine love and concern overtly. We need to come to terms with the wisdom of losing the battle to win the war. Our objectives remain the same. Sometimes, though, it takes a little longer to get there.

7) Crying: We must pray. I will never forget the tears and heartfelt cries of my dear mother of blessed memory, as she lit the Sabbath candles every Friday afternoon. (At least it helped my siblings.) We must implore G-d to grant us the wisdom to say the right thing at the right time, and more importantly, not to say the wrong thing at the wrong time. We must pray that we are able to control our anger; that we not allow our personal frustrations and moods to interfere with the commonsensical approach so crucial in raising children; that an

atmosphere of tranquility and joy pervades our homes, providing the security and warmth to nurture our children's optimal growth; that their hearts be open to fear and love of G-d, so that He bestow upon them all of His blessings, everlastingly.

Sheer Nonsense

Only in America:

1) Do drugstores make the sick walk all the way to the back of the store to get their prescriptions, while healthy people can buy cigarettes at the front of the store.

2) Do banks leave both doors open, and then chain the pens to the counters.

3) Do we leave cars worth tens of thousands of dollars in the driveway, and store our useless junk in the garage.

4) Do people order double cheeseburgers, large fries, and a diet Coke.

5) Do we use answering machines to screen calls, and then have call-waiting to ensure that we don't miss a call from someone we didn't want to talk to in the first place.

6) Can a pizza get to your house faster than an ambulance.

7) Do we use the word "politics" to describe the process of democracy, "poli" in Latin meaning "many," and "tics" meaning "bloodsucking creatures."

෴

Undoubtedly, there is much that transpires in our daily lives that is nonsensical and ludicrous, if not outright contradictory. Often we are so accustomed to our routines that we don't even notice a paradox in our behavior. Suffice it to say that were these inconsistencies limited to the physical realm, we could simply write them off as a product of the frailties of mankind. However, when such incongruity exists in the spiritual domain as well, we cannot simply dismiss it as irony, but rather must address it as a threat to one's religious potential.

Although it is wrong to play the blame game, undoubtedly we are, to a large extent, victims of our environment. We are ensnared and subject to the avalanche of its inundation. What used to be the television and the movies, or an occasional novel, has expanded to the DVD player, the iPod, and an all-consuming network of Internet communication that allows one to download anything and everything 24/7, no matter its poisonous content.

From promiscuity to violence, to simply living our lives vicariously through the lenses of others whom deep down we don't really idolize, young and old alike can easily be exposed to all that disrupts our natural desire to do what is righteous and to focus on the actualization of our inner selves. We are subject instead to enormous attention deficiency: the inability to focus at best, and the total loss of any focus at worse. We are guilty of transgressing a "prohibition" so blatant that it need not be written: the prohibition of "do not act stupidly." I know that I run the risk of being labeled a prude, yet I propose that in spite of the overwhelming sway of society at large, exposing oneself and one's children to such influences cannot be described in any other way. It is unwise, unintelligent, brainless, and imbecilic. In other words, it is sheer nonsense!

If we could be honest for a moment we would see that the entertainment center, proudly displayed in the living room as an integral part of the home, can be compared to allowing one's coffee table to house the most explicitly decadent magazines, without concern for who will enter the home and be seated in full view of such obvious depravity. "Oh Reverend, please have a seat in the living room. My husband will be right with you." Forget about the cleric! What about your husband? What wife, in her right mind, would be happy with her husband's unmitigated staring at other women, let alone the most exquisite in the world, dressed (hopefully), to kill (his eternity and perhaps their marriage), in a setting that provokes the emotion and stirs the heart. Will this encourage him to appreciate her more?

And forget about the husband. What about the children? Do they not absorb like a sponge? How dare we contaminate their pure minds with licentiousness and debauchery? How dare we tamper with their eternity? Have we lost our minds?

I know what we can do! We can move everything out of the living room into a place more private. Now we've lost it entirely! We're going to allow our family members to spend hours alone with their Internet hookup? Imagine how "knowledgeable" they will become with all that information at their fingertips!

Before we end up blaming everything on the wives, let us ask one more question. What's with the husbands? Where is their fear of Heaven? Where is their common sense? You don't have to be a rocket scientist to figure it out! There are many violations being transgressed, but one that stands out is the one mentioned above: "Don't be stupid!" To live a life of spiritual repugnance is a sure road to the unfulfillment of one's potential and will leave a person empty and hollow.

Years ago the television was referred to by some as the "idiot box." Presumably, that was because one could sit before it for hours and let his brain "fry." I think the expression is much deeper than that. There is much to accomplish in life. We need to use every precious moment to accrue merits to acquire our eternity. We need to blossom and expand, through a constancy and stability that will nurture that growth. We have enough problems with the inevitable ups and downs of life. We need not invite more upheaval and disruption.

We must not join ranks with the fools of the world and "box" ourselves into a confined existence – one that caves in under the influences of that which destroys us and denies our souls their natural expression.

Teenagers Forever

A woman who was celebrating her 104th birthday was being interviewed by the local news. "What, in your opinion, is the most phenomenal aspect of having lived one hundred and four years?" she was asked.

The old lady thought for a moment and responded: "No peer pressure!"

 C3C3&)ED

Much has been written about adolescents and the powerful influence their friends have upon them. The mesmerizing power of peer pressure and the strong need of the teenager to fit in can easily dominate those important developmental years. In those years of physical and hormonal change, the young not-quite-yet adult feels the insecurity brought on by transformation, and clings to friends going through the same. Much of this is to be expected, and the parent needs to make the proper adjustments to weather the storm and somehow maintain that balance between mentor and instructor (dare I say disciplinarian), and loving friend and confidant.

Some of the challenges parents face with their teenage children might find their foundation in Western culture, which does not rush the growing-up process, and allows for years of wallowing in an in-between state of "neither here nor there." In many other cultures, the maturing process can be quicker and less obtrusive. The words of our grandparents (or great-grandparents): "When I was your age, I was already working to help support the family," or "I raised all my younger brothers and sisters," are echoes of generations past, and don't exist in the world of the "swipe the credit card" teenager of today. (The story is told of the grandfather who said to his five-year-old grandson, "Why, when I was your age, I was six!")

The key word is the "R" word – "responsibility." It separates the men from the boys, and expedites growth and maturation. In no way does this imply that the playfulness of youth serves no purpose and needs to be eliminated, nor does it suggest that one rush by and ignore the natural developmental process of adolescence. Nonetheless, teaching our children to be people who assume responsibility would go a long way toward making the transformation of the adolescent years more spontaneous and self-generated.

Then there is the other extreme, the perpetual teenager who holds on to his playfulness well into his adult life. What used to be the bowling alley, miniature golf, or shooting pool evolves into the opera and Broadway, or season tickets at the ball park. "Hanging out" and "shooting the breeze" becomes clubbing and the bar scene, lavish dinners at fancy restaurants, and extravagant vacations. Thanks to an all-encompassing drug culture and a promiscuous culture, excessive playfulness and unwillingness to mature can get much worse, and much more pervasive. Unfortunately this "Peter Pan, I won't grow up, I'll never grow up" attitude pervades the world. Granted, even adults need their outlets and change of scenery, but not at the expense of grossly distorting man's mission in life and relinquishing his massive responsibility.

We must grow up! We dare not remain teenyboppers our entire lives, afraid of change and intimidated by our peers who might mock our spiritual growth – not only because of the emptiness we will convey to our children, but for our own sakes, for our own happiness, for our own eternity.

SPIRITUAL
Tools

Keep on Praying

Bugzy Goldberg, a notorious crook, was incarcerated at a maximum security facility for fifty years to life. His crimes included grand larceny, auto theft, kidnapping, breaking and entering, attempted murder, and murder in the first degree. One day he received a letter from his aging father, filled with expressions of his unconditional love for his son, and his overwhelming loneliness.

> Dear Son,
>
> I miss you so terribly! I remember, so fondly, how you and I would go outside this time of year to prepare the vegetable garden for planting. We'd plow up the ground, sow the seeds, and sit back and watch it grow. Oh how I long for those days. Now I'm left to do it all on my own and I hardly have the energy, let alone the willpower.
>
> All My Love, Dad

A few days later, Mr. Goldberg received a letter from his son Bugzy in prison:

> Dear Dad,
>
> Whatever you do, don't dig up the garden! That's where I buried all the bodies.
>
> Love, Bugzy

The very next day, two vans pulled up to the old man's home, and ten FBI men exited with shovels in their hands. For the next two hours, they proceeded to dig up every inch of that garden, but found absolutely nothing but dirt.

135

Two days later, the old man received another letter from his son in jail. It read:

Dear Dad,

By now, the garden should be all dug up and ready for planting. It was the best I could do under the circumstances.

All My Love, Bugzy

CS CR SO EO

In many situations in life, with our backs against the wall, we are ready to throw in the towel. Truth be told, though, one of man's greatest strengths is his resilience, his will to never give up. No matter the circumstances, a person must be steadfast in his belief that he can persevere. He should not relinquish hope, but should continue to implore G-d's mercy.

A person once complained to a famous Rabbi that he prays and prays for a particular matter, and he feels as if G-d is not listening. The Rabbi told him, "G-d is definitely listening, but for the time being, the answer is no." Often the answer is "not yet," but we must never become discouraged. We must continue to pray with the conviction that prayers are never wasted. One prayer pulls in another one. At the propitious moment, they will find their mark; they will make their impression, and then G-d will respond. Keep praying! Don't stop! And, most importantly, in the process, one will find oneself developing an ongoing, intimate relationship with one's Creator.

It is a grave error to think that one's prayers don't help, or aren't accepted because of one's sins. It isn't uncommon for a person to believe that G-d despises him. This is nothing more than a tactic of the evil inclination, who would like us to believe that we are unworthy. In truth, the very nature of prayer is such that if uttered with sincerity, it will ultimately penetrate all barriers and will be effective in bringing the desired results.

We must always remember that although the disguise of the natural world as we see it is so well done that we are deceived into believing that nature is something less than the miraculous, such thinking is our own folly. In truth, there is no difference between nature and miracles. It is all miraculous, as dictated by an All-Powerful G-d. For this reason, there is never a time when we should abandon our hope, for there is nothing "too natural" to allow for hopelessness. And there is nothing too miraculous for the Source of all miracles (including nature) to at times perform, even under the worst circumstances, in the most natural way.

Longevity

The old man had just finished one hundred sit-ups in view of a group of young men.

"Look at me!" boasted the trim and fit senior citizen, pounding a very flat and firm stomach. "Fit as a fiddle!" he bragged. "Do you youngsters want to know why? I don't smoke, never took drugs, I don't drink, I don't stay up late, I stay away from all sugar, and I don't eat meat!" The old man smiled at them, teeth white, eyes aglitter, and continued, "And tomorrow, I'm going to celebrate my 100th birthday!"

"Oh! Really? Celebrate?" drawled one of the youth. "How?"

❦

Long life is no doubt a marvelous gift, but if that's where it ends, then there's not that much cause for celebration. King David wrote in Psalms: "The days of our lives are seventy years, and with strength eighty years; their proudest success is but toil and pain, for it is cut off swiftly and we fly away." Were it not for our belief in the soul's immortality, the brevity of life and the ephemeral nature of its accomplishments would be disconcerting to say the least. The sadness of not seeing perpetuity to one's life-long endeavors can cause considerable despondency.

A generation that sinks its best years into destructive addictions in desperate pursuit of a temporary high is one that has already fallen into the clutches of depression. When the apex of life's potential is confined to this world, the reality of our mortality hits home and fills the couches of many a professional with the woes of our pessimistic

sense of inadequacy. How anyone can survive the inevitable tribu-
lations of life without a strong belief in the Afterlife is beyond me.
How fortunate are those who are steeped in this belief, and dedicate
their years in this world toward achieving eternity.

I distinctly remember the hundreds of days that I spent with my
father of blessed memory in various hospitals during the difficult
years of his illness (my father was hospitalized the last eighteen
months of his life). Most of that time, on a respirator and receiving
dialysis three times a week, the only way I could communicate with
him was by writing on a whiteboard. I would write the word "smile"
in big letters and my father would flash the most magnificent smile.
This gave my siblings and me – as well as some of the hospital personnel – tremendous encouragement, and an added resolve not to
lose hope and to continue the battle for his recovery.

Needless to say, I found it difficult to understand how a man
like him, an eminent scholar, totally incapacitated and dependent
on life-support, could still smile. I theorized that only a person who
understood the unequivocal reality of an Afterlife, and how every
second of life on this earth provides one with the opportunity to
expand that eternity – as my father well understood – could rise
to the occasion and even strengthen others under such horrific
circumstances. Knowing my father's deep faith allowed me to fight
off suggestions from hospital personnel that dialysis be stopped and
that "quality of life" become the creed that determines whether one
should continue to live or die.

As the government attempts to control healthcare, the notion
that the mores of society and its idea of medical ethics will prevail is a
frightening thought. Euthanasia and pulling the plug on life-support
machinery could become the rule rather than the exception. Refusal
to treat people of advanced age with costly treatments might be the
bottom line. When the determination of what constitutes the end
of one's life is left in the hands of mankind, we are in deep trouble.
Even more concerning is the imposition of a mindset that perceives
quality of life as something that pertains solely to this limited world,

without a thought to the steadfast belief of millions that life in this world is inextricably linked to, and acts as a corridor and preparation for, a life of real quality and meaning in the World to Come.

Indeed, for the many committed to this philosophy of life, every precious moment of life on this earth is worthy of celebration. The opportunity to build one's eternity through the effort of overcoming even life's most difficult challenges is reason for jubilation. Perhaps this was intended in the words of King David elsewhere in the book of Psalms, when he said: "Don't cast us aside to old age, don't abandon us when our strength wanes." Allow us to see and be inspired by the bigger worldview even as we wax old and are subject to the trials of the frail and infirm; allow us to be encouraged by the ultimate goal of achieving eternity, every moment of our lives.

Man's True Strength

UNITING THE FORCES OF ONE'S HEART CAN ACCOMPLISH THE IMPOSSIBLE.

A short, scrawny fellow interviewed for a job as a lumberjack. The foreman was unimpressed by his small size and barely acknowledged him, until the little guy pleaded with him to give him a chance.

"Okay, let me see what you can do."

The little guy grabbed an axe, and in ten minutes he had single-handedly chopped down an entire tree.

"How did you do that?" asked the foreman, wowed by his proficiency.

"Oh, I used to chop down trees in the Sahara Forest."

"You mean the Sahara Desert?" asked the foreman.

The little guy answered, "Oh, is that what they call it now?"

☙ ❧ ❦ ❧ ☙

We are a society enchanted with our physical prowess. Building muscles and biceps has become our obsession. How ironic it is that today's world, which so dramatically worships physical strength, has literally stripped man of his true strength. It has reduced the stature of man to that of a weakling incapable of achieving what he was intended to achieve.

The original dimensions of man as planned – which personified stretch ability, extension, and expansion, have been replaced by a self-oriented, featherweight mind-set, which incapacitates a person and prevents him from actualizing his true strength potential. The result is catastrophic and destructive. When evaluating true strength, one must conclude that it has very little to do with size, and very much to do with willpower, for nothing can stand in the way of willpower. It is that willpower that is the essence of the human spirit and can transcend all limitations.

As avid sports fans, we are well aware of the amazing feats an athlete can accomplish when the adrenalin is flowing, performance that seems to exceed his natural talents. By uniting the forces of his heart he seems to achieve the impossible and can produce results that transcend nature and surpass all physical expectations and limitations. Whether it is the unusual speed of the base runner attempting to steal second at the bottom of the ninth of the seventh game of the World Series with two outs and his team down by one run, or the leap in the air by the center fielder to rob the opposition of the winning run, there is no question that these feats are the result of tremendous willpower and drive to achieve a goal.

Man's ability to stretch himself and attain record accomplishments in the spiritual realm surely knows no bounds. With G-d-given adrenalin, even the sky is no limit. Such is the innate potential of man when he holds onto his true dimensions, unfettered by a self-oriented environment. The more he attempts to emulate his Creator, the more strength he is given to surpass that which limits others who aspire for less.

We must never forget that man was created in the image of G-d and inherently possesses the potential to act G-d-like in his interactions with others during the course of his life upon this earth. Therefore, just as G-d is compassionate so shall you be compassionate. Just as G-d is patient, so shall you be patient. Just as G-d gives life, so shall you give life. And just as G-d is omnipotent, so shall you strive to expand yourself without concern that it is beyond human capacity, for as a man created in the image of G-d, you don't know your own strength.

To Tell the Truth

THE ABILITY TO ADMIT YOU ARE WRONG LEADS TO A LIFE OF PERSONAL GROWTH.

The two elderly gentlemen, Harry and Isaac, were sitting in their doctor's waiting room, sharing information about their aches and pains, when they realized that each had the exact same symptoms in his foot. When Harry was called in, Isaac, remaining in the waiting room, listened intently, anxious to hear his friend's fate. Bloodcurdling screams were heard coming from the examining room, making Isaac even more anxious.

Finally, Harry came out and Isaac was called in. Harry, curious to see if Isaac's treatment would cause as much excruciating pain as his did, decided to wait for his friend so that they could compare notes. Two minutes later, Isaac was back in the waiting room, smiling from ear to ear.

"I don't get it!" said Harry. "We seem to be suffering from the same ailment, yet my treatment was so painful and yours was a breeze!"

"Harry," whispered Isaac, "do you think for a moment that, after listening to you scream in there for half an hour, I showed the doctor the right foot?"

છ૯૪૬૭૪૭

It's not easy to admit the truth. We're not particularly good at it, for many reasons. We are surrounded by, and submerged in a world of falsehood that inevitably takes its toll on even the most well-meaning amongst us. From the political spectacle of unkept promises and sensational hype, to the lack of commitment and fidelity in our most sacred relationships, mankind has shown himself to be nothing more than a self-serving fraud.

How distant we are from the world of the pious of the past whose steadfast and unrelenting commitment to truth was inextricably linked to their close attachment to G-d, the source of all that is true. By emulating Him, with full knowledge that His very signet and crowning symbol is truth, they pursued truth with alacrity and fled from anything that threatened their integrity. In fact, the Talmud says, "The pious cherish their money even more than their physical existence," the reason being not their enchantment with money, but rather their love of honesty and integrity and the relentless pursuit of truth that went into its acquisition.

Unfortunately, our attachment to truth and our ability to admit when we are wrong leaves much to be desired. I'm reminded of the story of a woman who hears a report on the radio warning drivers and pedestrians about a "crazy" man who is driving down the boulevard the wrong way. Concerned about her husband, who often takes that route, she immediately calls him on his cell phone.

"Hi! Listen, I just heard on the radio that there's a crazy guy driving down the boulevard the wrong way! Please be careful!"

"What do you mean a crazy guy?" he responds. "There are hundreds of them!"

I used to think this was a humorous story until I once mistakenly made a left turn into the wrong lane of traffic, and suddenly found dozens of cars coming at me at fifty miles an hour. It was quite frightening! I just pressed on that horn and hoped for the best. But what I found even more disconcerting was that my initial reaction was to wonder why all those cars were going the wrong way, until it hit me that it was I who was on the wrong side of the road.

My ninth-grade English teacher gave off an aura of confidence and assuredness mixed with a little pomposity and arrogance. He would boast: "I was wrong only one time in my life: I once thought I was wrong, when really I was right!"

We have a hard time being wrong in a world that preaches state-of-the art perfection and that it's not important whether you win or lose, as long as you win! Who could admit to the truth, when admitting one's mistakes is associated with failure and imperfection? And when you add to the equation a general malaise of low self-esteem, admitting our indiscretions becomes emotionally unbearable.

In addition, our general approach to things that are broken is to throw them out rather than fix them, so why even begin the process of "fixing" by admitting one's mistakes, when it is an effort in futility? It's been said, humorously, that there was a man from Los Angeles who had a watch that was always three hours fast. Rather than fix it, he moved to New York. Unfortunately, we've become a throwaway society, where appliances are made to break and leftovers are deemed inedible simply because they've spent the night in the refrigerator.

Much to our chagrin, however, we cannot simply throw out our "old selves" and buy new ones. We need to begin the process to be intellectually honest and introspective, with the greatest of integrity. If we don't make that move, we will never grow, and we will never change. We will just dig ourselves deeper into the pit that we created through our fraudulent behavior.

It is told that in a certain town where the Jews were victimized by various anti-Semitic decrees, the congregation accepted upon itself not a fast day and not a day of prayer, but thirty days of accepting criticism without uttering a word of defense or response. For thirty days, everyone was to acknowledge the truth, to admit and to absorb, and to allow constructive criticism to penetrate. What greater show of willingness to change could there be than to begin the process by connecting to the truth? Could there be a better way to prevail upon G-d to annul the evil decree? For when people attach themselves to truth, the stage is then set for sincere and earnest repentance.

THE WORLD
We Live In

Life Insurance

An eighty-year-old man enters an insurance agency in Tel Aviv and tells the clerk he wishes to purchase life insurance.

The clerk, trying to hold back his laughter, tells the old man, "You're too old. We don't sell life insurance to a person your age."

Unflinching, the old man says, "Well, two weeks ago you sold life insurance to my father."

"Your father! You must be kidding! How old is your father?"

"He's 108, may he live and be well until 120 years," replies the elder statesman.

"If you insist, I'll look it up but I highly doubt it... One minute... Why, you're right! I guess it's only fair that we sell you a policy as well. Can you come in next Tuesday for a physical?"

"Next Tuesday? No, I'm afraid I can't. You see, my grandfather is getting married next Tuesday!"

"Let me get this straight," says the incredulous clerk. "Your grandfather is getting married next Tuesday? My gosh! How old is your grandfather?"

"My grandfather is 132, may he live until 120."

"Your grandfather is 132 years old and he's getting married next Tuesday? Can I ask you one more question? Why in the world did he wait so long?"

"Ah! His parents are giving him a hard time!"

ෆ෨ඥෂ෩ෂ

From time immemorial, man has yearned to uncover the secret to longevity. Advances are made every day in medicine and technology that are increasing life expectancy. Emphasis on fitness, exercising, body building, and dieting has become routine for many, in their ongoing effort to maintain their youthful appearance and physical health. We have become a society who will undergo whatever ordeal necessary in order to shorten our nose, brighten our smile, remove our need for unflattering eyeglasses, and the like. Cosmetic surgery helps contribute to the myth that we can defy mortality and live forever. But deep down we all know the truth. The end is inevitable, and, unfortunately, by then the person who has chased after youth all his years will have wasted precious years of his life, dreaming the "impossible dream."

Not so for one who views the world through the spectacles of eternity. He knows that in the true spiritual world, life goes on forever. He understands that man is a composite of a body and a soul, and he strives to earn his eternity – not in some abstract, fictitious, and frivolous manner, but in a structured, deliberate, and concrete program of kindness and charity, honesty and integrity, and character refinement that will accrue the merits to allow him to live forever in the spiritual world. Indeed, authentic acts of integrity and kindness enable one to live everlastingly. G-d placed the fountain of youth and the secret of life in our very lap, and no one is giving us a hard time.

Shifting the Blame

A man was talking to the family doctor. "Doc, I don't know what to do. I think my wife is going deaf!"

"Calm down, now. Don't jump to any conclusions," said the doctor. "Let's test this thing out. This is what I want you to do to test her hearing. When you go home, as soon as you enter the house, ask her a question in a relatively loud voice. If she doesn't answer, move a little closer and ask again. Keep repeating this until she answers. Then you'll be able to tell just how hard of hearing she really is."

The man goes home and tries it out. He walks in the door and calls out in a loud voice: "Hello, I'm home! What's for dinner?" He hears no response. Moving a little closer to the kitchen, he tries again at the same decibel. "Hello, I'm home! What's for dinner?" Again, there's no answer. He repeats this several times, each time moving a little closer to the kitchen, but with no response.

Now, standing just a few feet away from his wife, he tries one more time. "Hello, I'm home! What's for dinner?"

"What's wrong with you?" his wife finally answers. "Are you deaf? For the eleventh time, I said we're having meat loaf!"

෴෴෴෴෴

Projecting one's own inadequacies onto others is a common aspect of the human psyche. Often such cognition is unbeknownst to the offender. Such "shifting the blame" can begin on a subconscious level, but with time can develop into a full-fledged attack, replete with slander and lies. It allows for a twisting and distortion of the facts on a massive scale. Historically, it has been the underlying cause of subtle (or not so subtle) outbursts of hatred and belligerence of the notorious and iniquitous, which have, all too often, evolved into full-scale persecution.

In recent times, the world has shown its true colors once again with its heavy-duty anti-Semitic response to an Israeli inspection of a flotilla bound for Gaza. The ship, with "supposed" humanitarian supplies, was no more than a provocation to break a legitimate and legal naval blockade. No nation in the world would be attacked for protecting its citizens by monitoring the access to a neighboring province whose declared intention is to murder innocent men, women, and children.

How ironic that those terror organizations who ignore the needs of their own people, and greedily hoard billions of dollars of aid for their own coffers, can even mention the word "humanitarian." How incongruous are the nations of the world in their oblivion to the Herculean humanitarian efforts of Israel in their defensive incursion into Gaza. Forced to enter these dangerous streets due to the bombardment and cold-blooded murder of their brothers and sisters – streets where terrorists hide behind women and children, in hospitals and infirmaries – Israelis nonetheless risk their lives to ensure that innocent Palestinians are not killed. At the end of that war, they pour in billions of dollars of humanitarian aid into the enemy camp, and yet, they are accused, by a world filled with cynics and detractors, of the harshest war crimes.

Shifting the blame is a common human defense mechanism that is antithetical to the coveted character trait of being "one who admits the truth." However, when combined with an irrational enmity that finds its roots in a true-blue envy, the results can be devastating. Nazi Germany began with such libel and slander, as did many a pogrom in the course of history. In recent times, the president of the world's most powerful nation, whose claim to fame was always that it was the world's defender of freedom and democracy, has chosen a path of "shifting the blame." It's always someone else's fault (for instance, the Bush administration, Wall Street, the oil companies, global warming, Israel, and the list goes on). Such a "scapegoat" attitude is frightening, for we know where it can lead, G-d forbid. May G-d save us from such evil.

Spiritual Suicide

A man went to see his rabbi with a major problem. "Rabbi, something terrible is going on and I must talk to you immediately!"

"What's wrong?" asked the rabbi.

"It's my wife. She's trying to poison me!"

"Your wife is trying to poison you? Are you sure?" asked the rabbi.

"I'm telling you, rabbi. It's no joke. She's trying to kill me. What should I do?"

"I'll tell you what. Let me talk to her and see what I can find out. Meanwhile, you stay on guard, and I'll call you next week," the rabbi suggested.

A week later, the rabbi called the man back. "Listen," he said. "I spoke to your wife. As a matter of fact, I spoke to her for over three hours. You want my advice?"

"Yes," said the man. "What should I do?"

"Take the poison!"

⚘⚘⚘⚘⚘

Only someone severely depressed or suicidal would take poison. An unsuspecting child might swallow a toxic household cleanser, prompting an emergency call to poison control, but any mentally sound, mature adult would know to steer far away from such danger. Yet many of us are guilty of ingesting all types of hazardous poisons and fumes in the course of our eating, drinking, and relaxation habits that threaten our well-being and that of others.

While widely publicized documentation about the dangers of the consumption of highly saturated fats, excessive cholesterol intake, and smoke inhalation (not to mention second-hand smoke) has impacted the behavior of many, nonetheless it has not stopped the general populace from indulging. Instead of taking the warnings of the Attorney General and other medical professionals seriously, they have flagrantly ignored common sense and exposed themselves, and others, to these poisons.

Our eating habits continue to be poor. The recent popularization of advertising campaigns that promote multiple types of eating with bright displays of every cut of meat or delicacy in actual size and color only exacerbates the problem. One particular steak advertised was selling for $80 a pound! It would leave the uninitiated with the impression that life is primarily about "packing it in" and "pounding the kishka." If it isn't a display of our gluttonous side, it certainly makes clear our detachment from a diet that is healthy and wholesome. Conventional wisdom dictates that if storeowners are spending the money on advertising, they must have the patronage and clientele. When will we learn that poisons are poisons no matter how delectable, and should be avoided at all costs? When will we end this "living in denial" approach toward life?

As much as guarding one's physical health from the many environmental poisons and dangers has spiritual ramifications as well, for the longer we live the more merits we can accrue, suffice it to say that there are genuine spiritual poisons we absorb that are far more dangerous, for they threaten our "eternal" health. These fumes are not limited to influences that seep in from the outside, but are even willfully brought into our homes. With full recognition that we live in a world that is by no means insular and that we fight an uphill battle to maintain our sanity, we must nonetheless not throw in the towel in a defeatist's attitude of hopelessness. We must marshal up the strength and the courage to ensure, to the best of our abilities, that our homes and schools are free of potential toxins detrimental to our spirituality.

Although we may argue that the world in its entirety is replete with danger (so who are we fooling?), we must know that for that very reason a safe haven in which to find refuge is critical, if not lifesaving. To allow the poisons of the streets, of technology, of Madison Avenue and Hollywood, to infiltrate our homes and our minds with the lame excuse of "Everyone else is doing it," or "If my children don't get access here, they'll get it somewhere else," is an expression of disbelief in our ability to swim against the tide. We must not live in denial, but must tune in, in a mature fashion, to the dangers that exist in our midst. To act in any other way would not only be irresponsible, it would be suicide!

EPILOGUE

Amaz(e)ing Savings

A man walks into a synagogue with a dog.

The attendant approaches him and says, "Pardon me, this is a house of worship! You can't bring your dog in here!"

"What do you mean?" the man responds. "This is a Jewish dog! Take a good look!" Sure enough the dog has a tallis (prayer shawl) bag looped around its neck. "Rover, I mean Reuven," says the man, "daven! (pray!)"

"Woof!" the dog barks, as he proceeds to open the tallis bag and take out a yarmulke, which he perches on top of his head. "Woof!" the dog barks as he stands on his hind legs, takes the tallis out of the bag, and wraps it around his shoulders and head. "Woof!" barks the dog as he then reaches for a prayer book, opens it up, and begins to pray.

"That's fantastic!" the attendant says. "It's absolutely amazing! It's just incredible! You should take him to Hollywood! Get him on television, into movies. He could make millions!"

"You try to speak to him," says the man. "I've tried until I'm blue in the face. He insists he only wants to be a rabbi."

ঙস্বেষ্ঠ৯৪০

It's not easy to get someone to listen to advice. Even the young and inexperienced can be defiant and stalwart in their insistence that they know better. In the world at large, the sagacious council of the older generation is not sought; instead of experience being an advantage, it is relegated to something to tolerate at best, and an added incentive to encourage early retirement at worst.

Such thinking is characteristic of a world gone wild. We must vehemently oppose such thinking, and always look to our elders and predecessors to be our guides, in our attempt to make our way through the woods and thickets of the formidable forest of existence. We look to our sages for inspiration, taking keen note of every detail of their holy and prophetic words. In the vernacular of my revered mentor and teacher in regard to the Sages of the Talmud: "We must bang our heads against the wall" to understand every word of their teachings, and the eternal lessons that lie therein.

A well-known parable makes this point abundantly clear. In years gone by, the ruling class would plant garden mazes around their palatial estates for the sake of amusement. Rows and rows of tall plants, bushes, and trees, identical in appearance, were arranged as walls between many straight and winding paths, all similar to one another. These paths either led to the gazebo in the middle of the garden, or led nowhere, with more bushes and trees blocking the way. Through trial and error, a person in search of the gazebo either found his way or, more often than not, got lost in the confusion of the indistinguishable environs, and wandered about in utter confusion. He could think he was on the proper path that led to the gazebo, only to find that path blocked as well, and that he had been mistaken the entire time. The walker among the paths of the maze had no way of seeing or knowing whether he was on the true or false path, as they all looked the same and presented no discernment to the observing eye.

However, the person who stands on the gazebo sees all the paths before him and can distinguish the correct ones from the false ones. He is capable of forewarning those walking through the maze: "Take this route! This is the proper path, take it!" Any person willing to place his trust in this individual will reach the designated place. But the person who is not willing to do this, and follows his own eyes instead, will surely remain lost, and fail to reach his destination.

The same is true in regard to the balance of life and establishing one's hierarchy of priorities and purpose. He who does not yet rule over his evil inclination is like one lost along the paths of the maze, unable to differentiate between them. However, those who rule over their evil inclination, who have already reached the gazebo, who have seen all the paths and where they lead, are competent to advise all those who are willing to listen. If we ignore that advice we will continue to wander in circles, without priorities and direction, entrenched in a maze of confusion. If we heed their advice, we will indeed merit "amaz(e)ing savings."

We are a GPS society that doesn't depend on anyone for directions. Self-reliant, with our apparatus plugged in, we do not need to know how to get to where we are going, or even the direction in which it lies. The GPS will do it all for us. In the end, we will get there without a trace of comprehension of which turns we took, and which turns we avoided. Most certainly, we would never ask directions from others. Not only might it leave the impression that we are so backwards that we don't own a GPS (Heaven forbid!), but we might transgress the unwritten rule of accepting advice from human beings, whom we can't simply unplug, and to whom we have to answer.

And although I am being somewhat facetious, this serves as a parable to our self-reliance and elimination of the council and advice of an experienced human being. One thing, though, rings clear. Even with this advanced machinery, there is no technology that can direct one lost in a forest. For that we must turn to the seasoned and experienced, the sagacious and the wise.

To wrap ("rap") it up:
Life is a daze
We are caught in a maze
Our hearts ablaze
A thick film of haze
Caught up in a craze
We need to appraise
To be introspective, to speak with a sage
So that we can gage
The source of our rage
Incarcerated, in an inescapable cage
A lost sheep, without grass to graze
We turn to the wise, to help properly praise
Our Father in Heaven, Who never ceases to amaze
All that contemplate His greatness, from the scrapheap
     He does raise
As we reroute our lives, and turn a new page.

It is my fervent hope and prayer that the ideas presented in these fifty-one essays – ideas that I was privileged to have absorbed from my many erudite and G-d-fearing teachers – serve as a source of inspiration to those who were kind enough to read this book. I hope that a smile was brought to your lips, and that the many layers of spiritual plaque that we allow to accumulate around our hearts were indeed penetrated, as "A Time to Laugh" turned into "A Time to Listen," and "A Bit of Wit" opens up "A World of Wisdom."